The Wild West Coast Of New Zealand: A Summer Cruise In The Rosa

Robert Paulin

THE WILD WEST COAST

OF

NEW ZEALAND.

A Summer Cruise in the " Rosa."

BY

ROBERT PAULIN.

WITH A FRONTISPIECE FROM A PHOTOGRAPH BY THE AUTHOR.

𝔏𝔬𝔫𝔡𝔬𝔫:

THOBURN & CO.,

136, SALISBURY SQUARE, FLEET STREET, E.C.

1889.

CONTENTS.

CHAPTER V.

CHAPTER VI.

CHAPTER VII.

CHAPTER VIII.

CHAPTER IX.

CHAPTER X.

CHAPTER XI.

CHAPTER XII.

CHAPTER XIII.

CHAPTER XIV.

AN EXPLORATION TO NEW ZEALAND—WEST COAST, SOUTH ISLAND.

CHAPTER I.

ON the 5th of November, 1886, C., O., and self left Dunedin by the 2.30 p.m. train for Port Chalmers. A good many friends were on the platform to bid us good-bye, for we were bound for what to most people, even in Dunedin, is almost an unknown land,—a part of the West Coast of the South Island, as yet but little known and seldom visited. The rest of our party, consisting of E., M., and three hired men (Danes) had preceded us to the Bluff—taking with them the stores and provisions; and at the Bluff the cutter "Rosa," 20 tons, which we had chartered for six months, was waiting to convey us and our belongings to the wild West Coast. For some days past we had been busy collecting stores, which chiefly consisted of flour, oatmeal, rice, sugar, candles, salt, tinned-meat, and a few dozen tins of marmalade, jam, milk and fruit—the luxuries to be used for high-days and holidays. We had also 20 lbs. of tobacco, and, in addition, 1,000 cigars, which I had recently received from a friend; a few cases of bottled London porter, which we hoped to find customers for; picks, shovels, hammers, cradles, sluice-box, tents, axes, blankets, cocoanut-matting, drills, fuse-coils, blasting-powder, guns, ammunition, fishing-lines, hooks, frying-pans, billies, porridge-pot and camp-ovens, tin mugs or panikins, as they are called, holding about a pint, and last, but not least in importance, anyway—matches. We

B

had also a case of chemicals and blow-pipe for testing minerals. Our oatmeal was in tins containing 33 lbs. each, and our flour in tins of 28 lbs. each—a precaution rendered necessary on account of the damp climate and the numerous rats which infest the West Coast.

Before proceeding further with the history of this journey I will give you some slight sketches of the individuals composing the party. M., C., E., O., and self went shares in the expenses, and there were in addition the three Danes who were paid wages. M. was almost a colonial, having come out to New Zealand when very young and being now about 27. He stood 5 ft. 10, was strongly built, had blue eyes and fair hair, long face and large nose, liked to be clean shaved with the exception of a small moustache, and possessed plenty of that self-reliance often met with in young colonials. His family occupied a good position, and he was quite at home either in stable, saw-pit, sheep-yard, stock-yard, or drawing-room. He was shrewd and very observant, and had had a good deal of camping-out experience both in bush and open country. Of him it was often observed—"That chap knows his way about." He had a defect, which as far as my experience goes, is more common among young colonials than British youth, and which is somewhat against their success as prospectors—he would work like a Trojan, and bear any amount of roughing, if he could see that good would come of it; but if the result seemed doubtful he would soon say it was not good enough and move off for something else—not exactly the stamp of man required for a forlorn hope. I have noticed this in many young colonials. Perhaps it is on account of their superior intelligence, which prevents them wasting their energies in vain; but certainly they soon loose heart unless speedily rewarded. They will not work long at poor claims on the chance of things getting better. If things go badly, and they get poor sport, it is more than likely they will not turn out again unless they hear of someone else's success. I had several instances of this during the trip, even when our circumstances were such that one or two birds would have been a welcome addition to the larder. Perhaps the reason is that New Zealand has been hitherto a land flowing with milk and honey; but now that the milk seems dried up and the honey is not easy to find, it remains to be seen how they will hold their own with others hailing from less favoured lands.

C. was an Englishman of Scotch parentage, an old Cheltenham boy, and had done a good deal of globe-trotting in Europe, Asia, Africa, America, and Australia. Some few years back he and a partner took up a sheep run in New Zealand, he having the money and his partner the experience. Alas, in a couple of years, let us hope he had the experience, but he certainly had lost both his money and his partner. He stood over six feet, was rather loosely built, of fair complexion, well educated, quiet, and gentlemanly, and as plucky as need be. About 30 summers had passed over his head and left it bright and shining—without any parting—a state of things the sand-flies and mosquitoes so seemed to appreciate that our friend when in camp generally found it convenient, for reasons of personal comfort, to sport a woollen night-cap. His brother E. was very unlike him, short, dark as a gipsy, quick as a needle, full of life and fun, wiry, energetic, not at all likely to pay too high a premium for his experience, a capital worker, and very useful in camp. He was always pottering about doing something or other, dusting, cleaning, or tidying, and observing that he was troubled about many things I called him Martha, and his brother I dubbed "the Squire." It is by those appellations I shall for the future speak of them. O. was a New Zealander of Scotch extraction. He was a hard worker, without a jib in him, not given to saying much, and a hard sticker to what he did say. He had the same fault as M. If good results did not appear quickly, he was for trying elsewhere. He gained the sobriquet of "Rameses," on account of an Egyptian-looking blanket that he slept in. He stood about 5 ft. 10, and was as strong as a bull.

Of the men, the eldest went by the name of Uncle Julius. By birth he was a Dane and had fought against the Prussian and Austrians. He left his country in consequence of the results of that war. He was a wiry, good tempered old fellow, of about six feet. Then there was Peter, a Fin, a strong young bullock of 20 years ; and lastly Samuel, a talkative, 5 feet 4 inches, wiry specimen of Danish humanity. He had previously been in my employ in survey work, and on that account he was now with us, but away from home he turned out a very bad bargain. In fact, as will be seen hereafter, the lot of them were rather chicken-hearted, and when they did not find nuggets on the beach to be picked up, commenced to sing so loudly for "*Dulce Domum!*" that a fortnight after we arrived at our destination we were glad to pay them off and send them home.

And now to return to Dunedin Railway Station. On the 5th of November, 1886, time 2.30 p.m., the last God-speeds are uttered by our friends, (a representative of the Press, I may mention, had the last word, for he stood on the step when even the train was in motion to offer me £1 a column for an account of our journey and adventures) and we are off to Port Chalmers—a distance of about six miles as the crow flies and nine by railway. The line follows the contour of the Bay all the way to the Port, save for about half-a-mile, the rails being laid only a few yards distant from high-water mark. By a succession of extraordinary curves the train skirts numerous Bays and the intervening Bluffs. On one side the traveller sees the Bay, about one-and-a-half-miles wide, and the Peninsula, with hills rising to an elevation of between a thousand and eighteen hundred feet, stretching beyond it. The hills of the Peninsula are of verdant green, dotted with houses, gardens, bush, and farms, and have a very pleasant appearance, especially on a fine day. The soil of the district is fertile, and enormous quantities of fruit and dairy produce could be obtained from it, were the land properly settled with an agricultural population. On the other side steep hills, mostly bush clad, come close down to the railway. The highest of them attains an altitude of close upon 2,000 feet. Occasionally a small valley opens out, shewing a few wooden houses, gardens and fields, but this side of the Bay is very much exposed to the south, and in winter is almost sunless. As a consequence vegetation is much later than on the Peninsula side. The Bay is very shallow, and at low water shews extensive mud-banks. The Dunedin Harbour Board have spent about half-a-million of money in dredging a channel from Port Chalmers to Dunedin, which is called Victoria, and in reclaiming acres of land about Dunedin, most of which is as yet useless. At present there is a depth of sixteen feet in this channel at low water, with a six to eight feet tide. Retaining walls are constructed outside the channel. When the Board started this work it was supposed that the channel would bring all the home ships up to Dunedin, but they did not calculate on the home trade being done by 4,000 and 5,000 ton steamers, and many people think it would have been much better to have spent the money in improving the Bar to the main ocean at Port Chalmers, an opinion in which I concur, for, had they done so, by this time the largest steamers could have come into Port Chalmers in perfect safety. As it is they now fight shy of it, and have almost given up coming to Dunedin, and go instead to Wellington, Auckland, and Lyttleton, much to the detriment of Dunedin. No one is to blame for this but the greedy merchants of Dunedin, who were anxious to have everything at their own doors, and terribly afraid of anything stopping at Port Chalmers. As the Harbour Board is composed almost entirely of Dunedin men, and only a small minority from Port Chalmers, the former had their own way, and succeeded in getting nearly all the money, some £800,000, spent in and about Dunedin and the channel. At all events, they now have their reward.

It took us 45 minutes to do our nine miles, and we arrived at Port Chalmers only to find our steamer did not sail for the Bluff till 7 p.m. As we get out of the train we see her at an adjoining jetty—a 2,000 ton boat, with a little black smoke wreathing upwards from out her huge red funnel. It was the " Manupeuri," one of the Union Steam-Ship Company of New Zealand's numerous and well-appointed fleet. We go on board, carrying our belongings, pass through the Social Hall with its piano and handsome couches and fittings, and descend to the elaborately fitted dining saloon, with its numerous tables and crimson-seated chairs, which, fixed to the ground, turn half round from the table to enable people to get in and out of them more easily. The saloon is nearly full of all sorts of people, many with bags and parcels in their hands, talking to the stewards about their berths, and to friends and others on the same subject. I am an old traveller, and know my way about the Union Company's boats as well as I know it about my own house. I asked my companions the number of their berths, which we had taken the precaution of getting marked on our tickets at the Dunedin office, and without troubling stewards or anyone, we went straight to them, and put our bags, &c., on our bunks. Then we had several hours to kill. So we left the steamer and wandered about the Port, "Rameses" going off to visit some friends who lived near at hand. There is not much to see at Port Chalmers. The town has a population of about 1,500, but things are very bad just now with the Portites. Since the Victoria Channel has been dredged, most of the coast steamers and home ships, which used to discharge and load at the Port, go up to Dunedin, although I don't believe, if the truth were known, it pays them to do so.   There is a substantial graving dock, capable of holding vessels up to 2,000 tons, and Government has authorised a loan for constructing a larger one, to accommodate the ocean-going steamers. When that is done the Portites hope for better things; meanwhile they have not much but hope to live on.   The Squire and I wandered through the almost empty streets, went into a stationer's shop and made a few purchases, talked a little with the proprietor, and then finally subsided into an hotel and had a glass of beer a-piece.   Here we remained, sitting in a somewhat doleful frame of mind, till six o'clock, when we went aboard our craft and had dinner.   While we were engaged in this more pleasant and very necessary occupation, the steamer was getting under weigh.   The dinner was good, and we enjoyed it perhaps rather more than we should have done had we not mournfully reflected that it was perhaps the last civilized dinner we were likely to sit down to for many months. Is it to be wondered at that, with such a prospect before us, our little party was extravagant ?   The Squire and I divided a bottle of claret between us, costing 4s., very much ordinaire, but infinitely better than any you are likely to obtain at the best hotels on shore in that clime at a much higher price, for the drink of the Colony of New Zealand is really the most abhorrent, noxious trash, whether taken in the form of beer, wine, or spirits. All are more or less chemical compounds, having but a slight acquaintance with the hop, the malt, or the grape.   This, it is only fair to state, is a condition of things entirely brought about by the heavy import duties levied by Government, and the quality has far more to do with the numbers drink destroys out there than the quantity consumed.   This is no exaggeration but a true bill, for the writer has seen and tasted through the length and breadth of New Zealand for the last twelve years. The breweries are full of brewer's crystals and glucose, and very little malt or hops do you see about the premises. Recently, when discussing the subject with a Dunedin brewer, he told me the chemical they used made their beer keep and gave it a better flavour, while at the same time it was very wholesome, and had much the same effect as dandelion. Likely enough, but let me ask who has any desire to drench himself with dandelion ?   Every wine, spirit, or beer merchant, in my opinion, ought to be forced to give an analysis of the article he sells, and be heavily fined if found that the article is different from the analysis. After dinner we walked about the deck, the evening being fine and the sea smooth. We cleared Otago Heads at sunset, and when darkness set in were gliding along over the rippling surface of the water, the coast of New Zealand, with its gloomy-looking hills, looming to our right, and to the left nothing but the open sea, or, to use the language of Byron :—

> The sea, the sea, the open sea,
> The blue, the fresh, the ever free.

I repaired to the smoking-room and smoked a meditative pipe before turning in—thinking chiefly of the wife and baby-boy I had left behind. The little one was just beginning to speak a few words.

Next morning at 6 a.m. found us just off Waipapapa Point, near to where the steam-ship "Tararua" was wrecked a few years ago. This point has to be rounded by steamers going to the Bluff from Dunedin. If they keep on too long before altering their course they will run on rocks about what is called Loby Island; whereas, on the other hand, if they alter their course too soon, they will run foul of the mainland. It is, in fact, to the unskilful mariner, a choice between Scylla and Charybdis. The "Tararua" did the latter, and became a total wreck. Early one fine morning she struck the reef off the point about 300 yards from shore. No danger to life was anticipated at first, and two boats were lowered and sent to look for a landing place; but the swell rose with the sun, and when the boats, having failed to find a landing, in an hour or so returned, the rollers were breaking all round the steamer and they could not get near her. A lamentable ignorance of the coast on the part of those aboard was responsible for the loss of life which followed; for, had the captain or his officers known it, there was, only a few miles off, a small harbour, where the boats could have landed passengers in safety; and as the steamer carried boats sufficient to hold all on board, all might have been saved by taking to them directly the steamer struck and making for the harbour. Again, as the weather was fine, had the boats been lowered at once and the passengers and others put into them and just pulled out to sea clear of the reefs and ground swell, (about a mile would have sufficed) and waited till help came, which would not have been more than six or eight hours at the most, as the accident was known on shore soon after it occured, and steamers were sent off at once from the Bluff, not thirty miles distant—had this been done, there would have been no loss of life. The life-boats, finding they could not reach the steamer, left her to her fate. One of them pulled out to sea, the proper thing to do, seeing they were on the direct track of vessels passing between Dunedin and the Bluff, and got picked up in a few hours by a steamer sent to render assistance. They fell in with a coasting craft—our cutter the "Rosa"—sometime before the steamer came, and would have been taken on board by her had there been any need. The other boat tried to land through the surf and got upset, one man being drowned. Meanwhile, things went from bad to worse on board the steamer. The sea began to break right over her, and by one's and two's and three's, as the day wore on, the unfortunate people on deck were swept away, to struggle without avail for a few terrible minutes, ere all was over, with the cold, green, rushing, roaring water, the choking white foam and the clammy, clinging, fathom-long sea-weed. Thus they were swept away in full view of many on shore, who, powerless to help, watched the last struggles, and heard the last cries of their fellow beings as roller after roller broke over the doomed ship. Before sunset only one out of nearly a hundred souls was left. He was a Maltese, and when nearly all was over, he took a child on his back, sprang into the sea, and swam ashore. Unfortunately the child was washed away as he came through the surf, and drowned. Truly a dreadful tale of the deep—an awful premium paid to inexperience! Immediately after the wreck the Government put up a lighthouse on the point; had they done so sooner the loss of the "Tararua" on Waipapapa point would never have been chronicled. Fine and calm was the morning as we passed the scene of the wreck and proceeded to the Bluff, the mainland to the right and Stewart Island a ahead. After a comfortable breakfast, I passed the time yarning to the Captain and others, and playing quoits made of rope about six inches in diameter, the object of the game being to see who could pitch the most into a bucket at a given distance. At about 10.30 a.m. we made fast to the wharf in Bluff Harbour,

CHAPTER II.

THE Bluff is capable of being made a good Harbour. It is the chief Port for Invercargill, a town of about 6,000 inhabitants, 18 miles distant, with which it is connected by rail. At present the channel from the sea is narrow and winding, with nasty reefs in places, which, combined with strong currents and the hurricane squalls to which the place is subject, make it not so safe as it might be, as one or two remnants of stranded vessels I have seen in passing up the channel testify.

Beautiful as was the morning, I expected a heavy gale before long, nature having all her signals for a storm out. I was anxious to get away at once so that we might make Port William in Stewart Island before it came on; and my first question to M., Martha, and the Danes, who met us on the wharf, was: "Is all ready for a start?" All was not ready. It turned out that the Captain and his men had no stores on board as yet, and, in fact, had no money to buy any, and were waiting for my arrival to get the necessary £ s. d. before they could procure them. Captain Hanning, our future sailing master, now made his appearance. Although I had seen his testimonials, which were very satisfactory, and had sailed in his cutter before, I had never seen him. He was a tall man, who would admirably perform his function as a model for Hercules. He possessed a well-formed head, covered with dark curly hair, a high, broad forehead, and a quick, dark-grey eye. I noticed he was lacking three fingers on his right hand, the result, I afterwards ascertained, of an accident in a saw-mill. Further, he was evidently a man of quick temper, and inclined to have his own way; had he been less so, there is but little doubt that he would be much better off than he now is, he having often held good appointments and lost them through giving his employers too much of his mind. He proved a magnificent seaman, with pluck which never counted the odds, combined with a thorough knowledge of his craft. He explained that he had no money, and that though he knew he could not claim the money for which he had chartered his cutter, self, and crew till the six months were up, still he had a wife and family at the Bluff, and he wanted to leave them something to go on with, as well as get some stores for himself and crew. I gave him what he wanted, and he went off to spend it. There are many men like him now about New Zealand hardly able to make a living, who are owners of or working coasting craft. A few years ago, before railways connected the chief towns, and when steamers plying between the different ports were much fewer than at present, a good paying trade was carried on by small coasters, chiefly cutters and ketches; but now their trade is gone, and their owners and those who lived by them are more or less reduced to poverty. It took some time to get the stores; so long that we had a mid-day meal at a shabby hotel—the best in the Bluff—and were waited on by smart-looking half-cast young women, for though Maories are rapidly dying out, there are still a good many about this part of the South Island, and many a British sailor has taken to himself a dusky-hided and supple-jointed aboriginal.

It was three p.m. before we weighed anchor. A few people on the Jetty gave us a cheer, which we heartily returned as we sailed away. The Captain's wife called out as we left the shore: "Good-bye Papa, bring back plenty of gold!" The crew consisted of an Irishman nick-named Patsey; a Dane, familiarly known as Tom; and an Englishman also called Tom, who sailed as cook. To properly distinguish them the last two were respectively known as Tom the Dane and Tom the Cook. Patsey was a comical little cuss; had a joke for everything, and also an inexhaustible stock of most astounding yarns. With our own party we numbered twelve—rather a crush for a 20 ton cutter—and I wondered how they would all shake down should we be many nights at sea. The wind was fair and fresh, and we were soon clear of the Harbour and dancing along over the green waters of Foveause Straits at the rate of about six knots an hour, having about twenty miles to go on a south-south-west course to Port William, Stewart Island. Our reason in going there was that we could make a much better offing from there to the West Coast than from the Bluff, for before we could get to the

West Coast Sounds we had to round Puysegur Point on the mainland. This point is about ninety miles from the Bluff and nearly due west, and the same distance from Port William, but nearly north-west; and as the prevailing winds are west or south-west, we could sail from Port William, where we should have a dead beat from the Bluff. Then again, there are no safe harbours on the mainland between the Bluff and Puysegur Point. So that once out to sea we had no alternative, should the wind be against us and a gale come on, but to fight it out or run back for shelter. There is also a strong current setting through the Straits from the west, and as nasty a sea gets up in a hurry as anywhere on the New Zealand Coast, and that is saying a good deal. Seeing the number we had on board, and most of them not sailors, the Captain and I agreed our most prudent course was to make Port William, and then wait a slant to run to Puysegur. I should myself have been inclined to have gone right round Stewart Island, and then, had a favourable wind blown up from the south, we could have run before it right up to Puysegur Point, which, from my old experience of the "Rosa" I knew she was well able to do, and as matters turned out I believe we should have saved time had we done so.

Truly, the coast between Puysegur Point and the Bluff is as ugly, and rocky, and dangerous as the world can shew. Washed by strong and varying currents, and swept by almost incessant south-west gales, and with enormous rollers, emanating from the South Pole itself, eternally thundering on its iron rocks, but few days in a year pass here without visitations in the shape of sudden squalls accompanied by heavy showers of rain always approaching to and often consisting of hail and snow. Woe betide any vessel that gets becalmed a mile or two from that shore! Each mighty wave, as it sweeps along, bears her nearer and nearer to destruction, till at last she is among the breakers, and then God be merciful to all on board, for forming a back-ground to this uninviting sea-board, shapeless, gloomy-looking mountains often for miles rise abruptly from the sea, clothed to above 2,000 feet with dark bush, their peaks seldom free from mist or clouds, but when seen shewing snow and glaciers. It was wise to give this coast a wide berth, and await at Stewart Island for fair wind and weather.

We sailed along merrily till the Bluff was about six miles behind us, when the wind chopped from north-west to south-west, and came on to blow with hurricane force. Sail was shortened and the cutter stood up to it well. The white horses grew rapidly, and the "Rosa" was soon swept from stern to stern by the salt sea foam. An unhappy expression now gradually stole over the faces of several of the company, and one by one they leaned their heads over the bulwarks. The sailors had been having more nips than were good for them before starting, and there was a good deal of confusion. The captain, who was at the helm, often fairly danced with rage as the men muddled the ropes. Once or twice he lashed the helm, dashed like a cat across the deck, did what the men were trying to do, and was back at the helm before you could say Jack Robinson. We were towing a good-sized whale-boat, which ought to have been taken on board before starting, and which now got full of water and kept us almost at a stand-still. So serious did matters at length look that the sailors asked the captain to run for shelter to the Island ot Ruapuke, which was a few miles to leeward. In language more forcible than polite, he told them he would take the cutter to Stewart Island himself if need be, and I believe he could have done so if the necessity had arisen. Just then a heavy sea tore the whale-boat adrift, and we saw her no more. I was glad when it happened, for we immediately began to make progress. It was evident we could not make Port William, but the Captain said he would make for Horse-shoe Bay, a few miles to leeward of it; that we were just getting out of the worst of the weather, and would shortly be under the shelter of Stewart Island, when the sea would get less. This soon came about, and knowing that the Captain had the vessel well in hand, and that both wind and sea were going down, I did not see the force of sitting up on the wet deck amidst occasional shower baths, and so sought the seclusion which the cabin afforded when we were about 10 miles from Horse-shoe Bay. I lighted a pipe—being quite proof against sea sickness—and busied myself with my note-book, occasionally putting my head up to see how we were getting on. Some of my friends tried to keep me company, but if the motion on deck was bad, that in the cabin was worse, and they did not stay long. They again sought the deck. All save Martha apparently became fixtures against the bulwarks, and their heads were occasionally to be seen hanging over the sides of the vessel. They were already having a surfeit of the pleasures of *mal de mer*. The cabin was about 8 feet by 12 feet, fitted with two bunks on each side, one on either side being a good, square compartment, while the remaining two tapered off to nothing close to the rudder. The cabin-fittings included a small locker and a looking-glass nailed over it, and a little stove the chimney of which pierced through the deck. In this locker were some bottles containing whisky, and the crew kept coming down in their dripping oilskins so often for a nip, that at last I had to interfere, and the grog was locked up. As we approached nearer to the wood-clad hills of Stewart Island the sea became smoother ánd our progress faster, and at 7 p.m. we got inside Horse-shoe Bay, and after a few tacks into still water. Here we dropped anchor, and no one seemed sorry.

Horse-shoe Bay is quite land-locked, and has all the appearance of a Devonshire cove, with its fringe of firm white sand and wood-covered hills encircling it. Scattered along the beach are about twenty wooden huts, most of them empty; at one time all were occupied, when the timber trade was better than it is now. By the time the anchor was down and the sails stowed it was getting dusk. · All but the captain, cook, and myself went on shore, taking blankets, provisions, &c., with them. They took possession of an empty hut, made a roaring fire, and proceeded to fill the inside man and dry their externals. On board things were not quite so comfortable, for the cabin-floor was a few inches deep in water—the well having overflowed. The explanation of this was, of course, that the "Rosa" was not tight and taut as she once was. A good deal of water had also come through the ceiling, and everything was more or less wet. We pumped out the water, swabbed the floor, &c., started a fire in the stove, fried some beef-steak, and had a comfortable meal, washed down with London porter of the M. C. and P. brand. After the meat the Captain and I lighted our pipes and started yarning. I first told him my mind about the exhibition of grog-drinking we had had, and he was entirely of my opinion. The fact though is that in these small craft the Captain is more a mate with his crew than their master, the crew being in reality partners, getting their wages out of the profits. However, we secured what grog there was left, and I had not to complain again on that score. The Captain shewed me his log, one entry being to the effect that when he picked up the boat of the ill-fated steamer "Tararua," he was positive that had the

boats put out to sea all on board would have been saved.
His log shewed that the day was fine. He also said, as I
have before mentioned, that had those on board known of
it, there was a good boat harbour five miles from the
wreck, where all could have been landed in safety. After a
good yarn, he took one of the best bunks and I the other, and,
rolled in our blankets, we were soon sleeping the sleep of the
just. Next morning was Sunday, the 7th of November. I was
up early and found it to be a beautiful morning, but with wind
south-west and squally, a big sea running outside, and a low
glass. I got into the dingy, jumped overboard, and had a
delicious swim, the water being clear and warm. After getting
into the boat again and dressing, I pulled ashore. I noticed
the Captain watching me rather anxiously while I was in the
water. He told me afterwards he wondered how I was going
to get into the boat again without upsetting the small craft;
but it is long since I learnt how to get into any boat when I
could get my hands on to her stern. I had a pull of about
half-a-mile to the shore, and landed under a rocky point, on
the top of which was an old building once used for curing
fish, but now deserted and tumbling to pieces. It was about six
o'clock, and from the bush came the pleasant songs of numerous
birds. Very sweet, bell-like, and musical are the notes of the
New Zealand birds, sometimes having such an effect as you
might expect to be produced from millions of tiny anvils
hammered by fairies with silver hammers. After making the
boat fast, I sauntered along a firm, white sand, which
glittered with scales of yellow mica having the appearance of
gold. It is sometimes called New Chum Gold, as, seeing it for
the first time, one can hardly believe it is not the precious metal
itself. There were numerous pretty shells lying about, of
which I gathered a few for those at home, thinking little
George would like them.

I soon became aware of the presence of those curses
of New Zealand called sand-flies—insects black in colour,
with two small wings, shorter and thicker in the body
than a mosquito,—in fact something like large midges. They
fly slowly and without any noise, settle on you, and driving a
hollow spear into your skin, suck away till their bodies are
swollen to bursting-point with blood, and then they go away.
Their bite is very irritating, especially if one is not accustomed
to them. All along the south and west coast, by the sea and in

the bush, they exist in countless swarms. Our tents were often black with them, and the misery they inflicted was very great. Their working hours are from the first ray of light to the last. I soon had a cloud of them about me as I walked along. I passed several huts, all empty but two, and entering one of the empty ones sat down for a few minutes and made a rough sketch of the Bay, which looked very pretty with its dark-blue water fringed with white sand, and encircled with green timber-clad hills between two and three hundred feet high,—and the "Rosa" at anchor about half-a-mile from shore, with a little white smoke curling from her galley chimney. I next proceeded to the hut occupied by our party, and pushing open the door saw various forms lying about the floor —two in bunks—rolled in blankets, and asleep. I gave a cry to wake them up, and in a few minutes several half-dressed figures sallied out, and made their way to a small creek handy for the morning's wash. Their ablutions were rather hastened by the attention of the sand-flies. A fire was soon blazing and breakfast attended to. There were plenty of planks about, and we speedily rigged up forms and tables, and made ourselves very comfortable. After breakfast, clothes were hung out in the sun to dry; some pottered about the beach; and others, including myself, walked over to Half-Moon Bay, a distance of about three miles, the track sometimes going round pretty little firm sand coves, and sometimes inland over hills from 300 to 500 feet high all covered with thick bush or furze, and trees that were from 60 to 100 feet high. The bush chiefly consisted of red and black pine, iron, totura-wood, gowai, tree-ferns, with a thick undergrowth of ferns and supple-jack. The beach glistened with yellow mica. The red pine or remu is a very graceful tree, with drooping foliage, something like that of the deciduous cypress which grew by the river at Beaulieu. The wood is a good deal used for house building, takes a fine polish, and furniture made from it has a fine appearance. It is not a very lasting timber. Black pine is one of the best of the New Zealand timbers, being strong and durable, and well adapted for piles, bridges and piers. The rata or iron-wood is a very hard, lasting wood. The tree starts life as a creeper; its vines creep up some other tree, and cover it from top to bottom, their leaves and flowers being so intermingled with the branches and foliage of the tree, that they can scarcely be distinguished.

The vines increase in size, and the tree they encircle decays and dies. The vines then unite and form a large tree with a solid heart. I have often seen huge rata trees with portions of the old tree they have killed not yet rotted out of the coils of rata vines around them. The rata has a small, pointed, glossy leaf, and a bright red flower. Some of the West Coast ranges of hills at that time of year when the rata blooms look crimson with its blossoms. Gowai, or kowai as it is called in the North Island, has something the appearance of a wattle, having a yellow flower. The timber is good and tough, but, as a rule, too small to be of much use. Totura is a large heavy timber, very lasting, and much used for piles and telegraph posts. The timber has a reddish appearance something like cedar. It has a small prickly leaf. The tree-ferns varied in height, some of the tallest being 30 feet, and the fronds six or seven in length. The supple-jack is of the bramble family; it grows in vines of about an inch in diameter, very supple and terribly strong, for you can hang on to them with perfect safety. Cattle often get tied-up by them, and unless cut down die of starvation. We had a pleasant walk, the day being warm with a nice breeze. Such out-crops of rock as we noticed were mostly of a decomposing grey granite, with veins of quartz a few inches in thickness shewing here and there. Under the glass some of the quartz shewed masses of beautiful red, purple, and emerald crystals, with a speck or two of gold.

CHAPTER III.

HALF-MOON BAY has much the same appearance as Horse-shoe Bay, except that there are about 100 people living about it, and a good many houses standing, some of them being of decent size and having a comfortable appearance, with paddocks and gardens attached. There is a church and school, a saw-mill, and a small ship-building yard, where cutters are chiefly built. One of about 8 tons was on the slips at the time of our visit. Most of the inhabitants were in church when we arrived, but a few were about. One of them, a half-cast, having a smart, well-to-do appearance, got into conversation with us. He was known as Captain Steven West, and had been a great deal on the West Coast gold digging and sealing.

He said that at a place he knew of, near Jackson's Bay, he and another man once made twenty ounces of gold in a week. They worked with a cradle and trough, filling the trough with water at high-water, and washing out the sand which they got at low water. This they carried up to the trough and passed it through the cradle—the gold being in the sand. At one place, he assured me, they could rely upon getting six or seven ounces of gold after every heavy sea and high tide. He guessed who we were, as the fame of our West-Coast party had got noised abroad. On hearing of the loss of the whale-boat he said we could not do much without one, and that he had a good one he would sell. I knew one would be very useful, and told him I would talk it over with Captain Hanning and let him know. The gold he got was mostly in thin flattened pieces, sometimes weighing as much as half dwt., but he said they could only get it on the beach; as soon as they went inland they found none. We returned to Horse-shoe Bay after chatting with several other inhabitants. At one house we went to I tried to raise a drink, but they viewed us with suspicion and would supply nothing but water. On returning, the sun was quite hot, and I could not resist the temptation of having a swim at a pretty little cove we came across. It was most enjoyable, and a breeze from the sea had put to flight, for a time at least, the brutal sand-flies. The wretches go into the bush directly a sea-breeze comes on; but reappear the moment it dies away. We got back to our quarters at about 3 p.m., and wandered about talking to the new settlers who live around Horse-shoe Bay. Their lot did not seem a happy one. They had no gardens, and lived by doing a little wood-cutting and fishing, and sometimes going over to the mainland when shearing was on. One man, however, proved to be an exception to the general rule, for he was the fortunate possessor of a cow or two. The hills round the Bay are chiefly composed of decomposing granite. The tracks through the bush are well made, being formed of trunks of tree-ferns, placed crossways, and packed close together. The steep gullies and creeks were all bridged. A heavy south-west gale came on in the evening, the wind raising columns of spray in the harbour. I returned to the cutter about 6 p.m., having a hard pull back, and spent the evening in the cabin writing and talking to the Captain.

The next day was fine but squally, and a big sea outside; so after breakfast we started to explore the interior. We walked through the bush for five hours, following a well-made track, laid with wooden rails. The numerous gullies were spanned with well-constructed bridges, now very much decayed and rather dangerous to cross. There are many of these tramways in Stewart Ireland, constructed for the purpose of bringing timber down to the coast for shipping; but the timber trade, as I have previously remarked, has almost ceased, and the tramways have fallen into decay. An immense amount of labour has been expended on them. I doubt if they have ever paid for construction. One reason for this decay in the timber trade is that railways have now opened up timber districts much nearer the centres of population, those who are in authority over us having, in their wisdom, constructed the New Zealand railways all along the sea-board, and leaving the interior alone. From Invercargill to Christchurch, a distance of about 350 miles, the railway is never more than a few miles from the sea, and generally close to it. At present it does not pay to ship timber from Stewart Island. Some day, as the other sources get gradually used up, Stewart Island will be again resorted to, and her at present silent forests echo once more to the sound of the axe and the saw.

All this day we were never out of the bush, which, indeed, covers nearly the whole of the Island. We came upon several intrusive dykes of hard grey basalt, but got no traces of minerals other than iron-sand, which seems to be present everywhere. We shot a few pigeons and kakas. The pigeons are fine birds, larger than but having much the same plumage as the British wood-pigeon. The kakas are parrots; their bodies do not weigh more than that of the pigeon, though from the amount of feathers they have you would think they were larger. The plumage is brown relieved by red about the wings and tail; like all the nesters they are good eating. They go about in flocks, and should you wound one of them it will probably start screeching. Thereupon all its companions will come round, apparently to see what is the matter, and you can shoot at them as long as you like without driving them away. Some people can imitate their cry well enough to bring them round about them, should there be any within hearing.

We returned to our quarters at about 6 p.m. A heavy thunderstorm came on, and I amused myself by fishing from the cutter. I caught a dozen of white-fish and a lot of fine red cod. The white-fish are in shape like a roach, with small heads and mouths, white scales, and a brown stripe across the shoulder. They bite very shy like roach, and are caught best with a small hook. Their flesh is white and firm, and they are excellent eating. When caught they make a peculiar noise, something akin to the squeaking of a mouse. They ran from ½lb. to 4 lbs. weight. At the outset I was the only successful angler, for my companions, accustomed only to the coarser sea-fish, could not hook them. I think my roach fishing at Beaulieu may have had something to do with my success. In a day or two the others got into the knack of catching them; but at first they got rather riled when they saw me pulling them up and they themselves meantime solely occupied in losing their bait. Rock-cod are very much like rock-cod at home, with dark scales on the back, white belly, red fins, and enormous heads and mouths. Their flesh is soft, but they are not particularly good eating. Furthermore, we found them rather a nuisance, as when they were about no other fish except a dog-fish or young shark had a chance of getting at the bait, and after awhile, when we found red-cod about, we left off fishing. They are extremely voracious. They often weigh eight or ten pounds, and sometimes even more. Fortunately they did not come on the feed as a rule so early in the evening as the white-fish.

A very stormy night, with thunder and lightning and heavy rain (barometer 29·00), ushered in the following morning, which was the anniversary of the Prince of Wales's birthday. The Captain hoisted what bunting he had, and we drank his Royal Highness's health in London porter. The weather was still very wild, with a strong south-west gale and cold showers. I had my usual swim and enjoyed a breakfast of white-fish very much. I stayed on board till about 2 p.m., and then landed and took one of the men with me prospecting. Prospecting, I may explain, generally consists in digging a hole till you come on solid clay or rock, and washing the stuff you get out in a flat, shallow, iron or tin dish—you wash away the mud and earth and pick out the stones, and at last the minerals, if there are any, remain at the bottom. The formation about Horse-shoe Bay was so broken and loose that we found it difficult to get on any firm bottom. Wherever we tried we got large quantities of magnetic black iron-sand; on many beaches about Stewart Ireland there are considerable deposits of it. It is often called Titanic iron-sand, and is said to contain nearly seventy per cent. of pure iron. It owes its origin, I should say, to decomposed volcanic masses. There are large quantities of it at various places in New Zealand, perhaps the most extensive known deposit being at Taranaki, on the West Coast of the North Island. It is chiefly found there round about the base of Mount Egmont. Egmont itself is a beautiful volcanic cone 8,000 feet high, and the sand has, I think, doubtless been washed out of the mountain. A good many attempts, costing large sums of money, have been made to smelt it, and although fine metal has been obtained, the process has been too costly to allow the works to be continued with any prospect of profit at present. Some day, I have no doubt, it will be utilized. I believe there are enormous deposits of the same mineral in Iceland.

The 10th of November opened with a howling gale after a night of heavy rain, some of which found its way through the roof of the cabin. We spent the morning in overhauling the cargo and having things properly stowed, so that we might be ready to start as soon as the weather moderated. The Captain went over to Half-Moon Bay to inspect West's whale-boat, and came back and reported it to be a good one. So I bought it, the price being £6. The Captain deposited £1, and signed an agreement to the effect that the boat was to be mine as long as I wanted it, and that he would take it off my hands at cost price when my requirements ceased. He and three men walked over to West's carrying oars with them, and rowed back in the boat. She is a pretty model and pulls very easily. I shall take care that this one is properly looked after. During the day I started the men sinking a shaft, I examining the stuff every now and again with a magnifying glass and washing it in a tin dish. We sank down 10 feet and got on granite, soft at first and hardening as we went on, but found nothing but a few small pieces of soft white metal which cut easily and looked liked bismuth. The formation is a likely one for tin. It has always been supposed that there is tin on Stewart Island, but as yet it has not been found. Later on, the glass rising and the weather looking finer, I instructed those on shore to have all their swags packed up, and to be ready to go on board by daybreak. Then I went on board and spent the evening fishing, and again succeeded in catching a large quantity of fine white-fish. Not an unpleasant life this, but as we were anxious to get to Big Bay as soon as possible, this delay was annoying, and besides the men were getting wages and doing nothing for the money. These Danes did not seem to know how to do the simplest cooking, and their attempts at baking were simply horrible.

The 11th of November broke cold and fine. The hills—of which Mount Anglem, 3,200 feet, the highest hill on the Island, is the centre—were covered with snow to within 1,500 feet of sea level. I had my swim before the sun was up, and we all got on board and up anchor at 7.30 a.m. The glass was 30·16 and we hoped we might get right away to the West Coast; but we were not well out of Horse-shoe Bay before it.

came on to blo` hard from the south-west, so we had to
reef sail and make r Port William, arriving at 10.30, after a
hard beat.

Port William is a beautiful white-sanded bay, encircled by
bush-covered hills, closely resembling those to be found at
Half-Moon and Horse-shoe Bays. As we entered its still
waters we saw before us, fronting the shore at the head of the
bay, a long, low, wooden building and a small house to the
right of it, the only buildings to be seen. We anchored and
went ashore. The long building we found to be empty, and
in a dirty, delapidated condition. It was put up some years
ago by the New Zealand Government as barracks for 150
Shetland and Orkney Islanders, who were brought here at the
Government expense. They were given land, tools, and provisions for eighteen months, and it was supposed they would
clear and cultivate the country, and form a flourishing settlement, developing, among other things, a fishing industry, as
the sea round Stewart Island swarms with fish. The scheme
did not work well. The settlers did a little clearing—very
little—and then nearly all of them left, and made once more
for the main land. Thus the place was abandoned.

Garden flowers, fruit trees, and berry bushes still flourish
among the wild growth that has sprung up around them, and
show, by their healthy vigour, that with a little cultivation they
would give good returns. About half-a-dozen gum trees that
were planted by the islanders are now large ones, and will
soon tower above the surrounding timber. Gum trees
(Eucalyptus) grow at an amazing rate in New Zealand. I
have seen them cut down when but ten years old, and measure
ninety feet.

We were proceeding to clean out one of the rooms in the
barracks, preparatory to occupying it while we remained in the
Bay, when a ragged-looking individual, with red hair and
beard, light blue eyes, and a pleasant expression about his
face, made his appearance. He besought us to take up our
quarters at his house—the one we had noticed to the right—
where he said we could use his kitchen, and be clean and
comfortable. I did not like to intrude so many on him, but he
seemed to wish it so much that I consented. So we took our
swags to his house, which consisted of two rooms, one with a
large open fire-place at the end of it. He was known as Deaf
Dick, and was the one solitary inhabitant of Port William.

His only companions were an old-fashioned-looking Skye terrier and a cat. They sat one on each side of him, and seemed almost as if they were conversing with him. We dubbed them "The Familiars." I may here say that the Captain and his men owned two mongrel retrievers, one called Jack, a splendid swimmer; and our party had a tiny little wiry-haired Scotch terrier called "Fan." This little animal M. and "Martha" had bought for five shillings just before leaving Dunedin. She had evidently been a ladies' pet, could walk on her hind legs, and do other tricks. Probably the man who sold her to them had stolen her. She was always shivering, and had a hard time of it. At first she would not eat fish, and evidently expected more dainty fare. She attached herself to me, and followed me about like a shadow. Dick gave us food and tea, and shewed us his household gods. He is a bit of an artist, and produced a "picture," representing CHRIST on the Cross, of which he was the manufacturer. The outlines of the figures were cut out of cardboard, with a background of colored tissue paper, so that when you held it up to the light the Cross and CHRIST stood out, surrounded by various colors, the whole having a very pleasing effect. He also shewed us a bridle of plaited hide, very soft and strong, made in Mexico. He had lived in that country, and we were informed by him that such bridles were in common use out there. They are made from the skin of unborn foals, the mares being killed to obtain them. The workmanship was very fine, and the strength something remarkable. Dick has been most of his life a gold-seeker, and has sought the precious metal in America, Australia, and New Zealand. He is now, I should say, quite sixty, and worn and feeble-looking. His life would make an interesting book. Although he has had thousands of pounds in his hands, like many other old diggers I have met, he could not keep it, and now has nothing. He gets a little gold about the beaches near Port William, and with that and a little help from chance visitors ekes out his lonely existence.

After dinner the whole crowd went prospecting on the beach. We got a few colors of gold in every dish we washed out. The entire formation is a broken-up jumble, and did not strike me as being likely to contain much of anything, although it might, and doubtless does, contain specimens of various minerals. Dick's garden, which he keeps in good order, is about half-an-acre in size, and contains apple, pear, plum, and cherry trees, currant and gooseberry bushes, potatoes, onions, peas, lettuce and cabbages, all looking well and healthy. He spoke of two gold reefs he knew of, but said he was a poor man, and offered, if I would give him 12s. a week, to drive a tunnel into the hill where they were, and open them up. I asked him if he had ever seen any gold from them? He said no, but he knew those who had. I did not close with his offer. We found the reefs ourselves afterwards, and could discover no signs of gold in them. There were, however, masses of coarse-grained granite everywhere, intersected with veins of quartz and bands of fine-grained granite. Sometimes, too, we came across a crystalline metamorphosed sandstone. It is very hard, and would doubtless take a fine polish. It resembled very much the criffel stone in Scotland, of which curling stones are made. The day closed wet and stormy, with violent westerly squalls which made the water whistle and the cutter swing at her anchor half round the compass. All our party, except myself, slept at Deaf Dick's, and were made as comfortable as he could well make them. One drawback to comfort in the day-time in Dick's hut was, that if you shut the door, you were soon half choked with smoke; while, if you left it open, swarms of sand-flies came in and stung you. Dick gave our Danes lessons in cooking and baking, but they either could not or would not learn. I have come to the conclusion since that they did not want to, thinking that we would do the baking ourselves sooner than eat the awful abortions in the shape of bread produced by them, and so we did. We, however, sent our Danish friends about their business as soon as we had a chance.

Dick told us a number of yarns during the evening. He speaks with a loud voice, somewhat like a street preacher. The moral of his yarns was "that no one, however much his experience in prospecting, should ever leave a new place untried, even though its appearance little warranted the hope of finding gold." One yarn was to the effect that, once in Australia, he and a lot of other men, mostly old hands, were working in a gully. Dick's own mate was a new chum, who had had no experience whatever in gold seeking. They were getting very little gold, and the old hands had come to the conclusion that there was very little gold left in the gully, and had decided to leave it and try their luck elsewhere, Dick amongst them. Dick's mate, before they left, told his companion he was determined to go and try a slip he could see on a hill face across the gully. The only encouragement he had from the party was to be informed that he would be a fool for his pains. However, the man was obstinate and went by himself, and started working on the slip. In a very short time he came on gold in large quantities. Instead of keeping his good luck to himself, and making a considerable pile before his discovery was found out, which he might easily have done —for no one would have troubled to go near the so-called fool—he at once went back and told the others of his find. A rush was at once made for the reef, and this find of the obstinate new chum proved to be one of the richest finds in Australia. I returned to the cutter as night came on, leaving the others still listening to Deaf Dick's interesting yarns. It was rather hard work pulling off to the cutter, some of the squalls being very violent.

The 12th opened fine, but with a falling glass, barometer standing at 29·70, wind hot and puffy from the north-west. We walked to a place called Maori Beach, distant about five miles, Deaf Dick accompanying us as guide. A good deal of gold is said to have been found about this beach. There was no distinct track, and after wandering a good bit our party got separated, the "Squire" and "Rameses" keeping with me, and the rest going with Dick. I had taken the bearings of Maori Beach before we started, and, finding no track, steered a bee-line for it by the help of the compass. At first we had a little hard work forcing our way through the bush, which, as usual, consisted of pines, totura, ironwood, broadleaf tree-ferns, and a dense carpet of ferns and creepers, rotten moss-covered timber helping to make the way rougher; but presently we found ourselves on a very good track, and came to the conclusion that Dick did not know much about the country, for it was evident that this track came from near where we had started and went to Maori Beach. All was now plain sailing, and we soon found ourselves by a river which bounds one end of the beach, and crossing it by a bridge about a mile from the sea, we arrived at Maori Beach, which proved to be a sandy flat, covered with scrub extending inland some miles, and lying between two small rivers which enter the sea about two miles apart. We had our lunch, but were very much troubled by swarms of bloodthirsty sand-flies. We were presently joined by the rest of our party, who had not been so fortunate as to discover the track, but managed to do without it. We proceeded to the further end of the beach, but no sooner had we reached the river than the rain came down in torrents. Some were for going back. However, we decided to wait an hour or two and allow the tide, which was nearly high but ebbing, to go out, so that we could try a prospect in the bed of the river. Along the sandy flat by the beach we found several patches of strawberry plants growing among the grass, looking very healthy, and with plenty of fruit as yet quite green. We also saw signs of civilisation indicating that not long ago there had been a few settlers on the beach. The rain kept on steady and heavy, and, being unable to find any cover, we were soon drenched to the skin, and stood against such small timber as there was for shelter. In this fashion we patiently waited in wet misery for the water to fall. Suddenly we were hailed·by a cheery voice, and saw an oil-skinned figure, with a cheerful, amply-bearded face, emerge from the bush close to us. It proved to be a Mr. Thompson, from Half-Moon Bay. He was looking after some cattle which had gone astray, and doing a little prospecting at the same time. For the latter purpose he carried a pick on his shoulder. He told us he had heard of our party, wished us every success, asked us over to see him, and then giving us a cheery good-day, went about his business. We heard him singing away for some time after he had disappeared in the bush. In a couple of hours the tide had run out sufficiently for our purpose, and we commenced operations. Veins of quartz a foot thick and more were common enough, but it all seemed blind, nor did we get the colour of gold in washing. The rain kept on, and after an hour's steady work we gave it up and returned to Port William. We went home quicker than we came, at one place saving about a mile by walking through a river instead of going up its banks till we came to a bridge, as we had done in coming. For my part, seeing I could not possibly get any wetter, I would have swam the river if need be, sooner than wade the extra mile through the soaking bush and slippery ground. It is decidedly hard work climbing a steep bush track in New Zealand, when that track partakes of the nature of a watercourse; when your well-soaked clothes cling to your limbs with the weight of lead; and when the surface is greasy, and your feet slip about in dark, squashy, peaty soil, mixed with clay, wet rocks, and rotten decayed timber. It is indeed hard work, especially when one is not used to it, and so many of us found it to be, for drops of perspiration mingled with the streams of rain which trickled o'er many a manly brow.

At last it was over, and we arrived at Port William. Wet clothes were taken off and wrung out, but the lower garments were so stained with the black bush soil that it was deemed best to put them into clean water for the time being. I went on board, and was soon in that happy frame of mind and body produced by violent exertion and a soaking of several hours' duration in the cold, pitiless rain, followed by dry clothes, a comfortable seat and a good meal, all of which, with the help of the Captain and cook, I soon enjoyed in the "Rosa's" little cabin. The rest of the party did much the same at Deaf Dick's.

Over our pipes the Captain and I discussed the chance of the weather clearing up, for we were anxious to get away and be at the West Coast as soon as possible. We knew that, so far as the object of our expedition was concerned, it was sheer waste of time staying at Stewart Island.

CHAPTER IV.

BAROMETER 29·60., and a stormy night. Next morning it was worse, and the whole company seemed out of sorts, From Captain to cook every face looked glum, except Patsey, who is one of those sons of the Emerald Isle who laugh at fate. One can put up cheerfully with very little in the shape of creature comforts if occupied; but it is a different thing having to be content with a minimum of comfort, a maximum of idleness, and millions of New Zealand sand-flies.

A thunderstorm enlivened the scene at night. I spent the evening fishing from the deck and caught a quantity of white-fish, trumpeters and blue cod. The trumpeter is shaped much like a white-fish,. but rather darker in the scalés, and running to a heavier weight. It is about the best eating of all the New Zealand fish, and has a flavour not unlike salmon. Its flesh is too rich and contains too much oil to fry. The largest I have seen caught weighed about 12lbs., but I believe they are caught much larger, scaling as much as 27lbs. The blue-cod looks very much like the British cod, and runs from two to six or seven pounds as a rule, but in the sounds they often run to a far more considerable size. They have enormous heads and jaws, and bite very freely. They are very fine eating, their flesh being firm and white, with a good sea flavour. It was a pretty sight that evening as I sat alone fishing on the deck in my oilskins. Wild and picturesque was the picture presented by the white sand beach, the dark bush-clad hills in the background, with the heavy thunder-clouds resting on their tops; the only signs of man's presence being the deserted barracks and Deaf Dick's house, from the wooden chimney of which white smoke was curling upwards. As night set in the land seemed to fade away. Occasionally its outline could momentarily be seen as a flash of lightning broke through the Cimmerian darkness and lighted up the landscape around. When I turned in our little cutter was swinging uneasily at her anchor, and a moaning swell, caused by the heavy sea outside, was breaking on the beach.

The 14th was still stormy, with a falling glass. It was Sunday. I pulled myself ashore in the little dingy, and going to a small cascade near at hand, sat under it, and had a fine fresh-water shower-bath, the sand-flies being unpleasantly attentive meanwhile. Some of our party came along for the same purpose. The morning ablutions over, we adjourned to Dick's for breakfast. When the meal was finished and cleared away, Dick laid on the table a Bible, some Salvation Army publications, some old *Good Words*, and a volume of *Sunday at Home's*, dated 1862, and taking up one of them sat himself by the fire, with his animal pets on either side of him. There was something in the old man's manner which induced all of us to follow his example, though to some of us such a way of spending the Sabbath was not usual. Thus we sat, occasionally smoking, till 3 p.m., when we had dinner off a magnificent trumpeter, weighing about 12lbs. After dinner there was more reading and smoking, and about 5 p.m. I went on board our craft. A small lugger, called the "Reindeer," manned by one man, the owner, and a boy came in and anchored alongside. She was a curious-looking vessel, with high, stiff bulwarks, which looked as if they had been made from planks from packing cases. She would be about three tons. Her owner was a red Scandinavian, with long, rough hair and a rugged face, in which eye-brows, whiskers and beard seemed to blend together. He and the boy came on board the "Rosa," the boy remarking "Ah, this is something like a ship." They get their living chiefly by fishing and oyster dredging, the Stewart Island oysters being among the finest in the world, a little larger than, but in taste and appearance quite equal to British natives. I noticed that the other man, who remained on board the "Reindeer," did

not return our Captain's salutation, and remarked on it.
" Probably not," grimly said the Captain, " I gave him one of
the best hammerings he ever had not long ago." There the
subject ended.

The wind shifted in the evening and the glass began to
rise, giving us hopes that the weather would mend before
long. The Scandinavian, however, said it would not clear for
some days yet. He also mentioned that the gale we had
encountered in coming over from the Bluff was one of the
most severe that had been known for some time, and that there
had been doubts about our safety in consequence. The next
day was worse, and the succeeding one, the 16th, was no
better.   We decided, however, to change our quarters to
Half-Moon Bay, with a view to supplementing our provisions,
so we weighed anchor about 8 a.m., and after a hard beat out
of Port William, close reefed, we scudded down to Half-
Moon Bay, arriving there about 11.15 a.m.   Deaf Dick, as he
shook hands at parting, said, " The Lord bless and preserve
you in your going out and your coming in.   The Lord be with
you and guide you on your journey."

Half-Moon Bay is very like the other bays we had visited ;
only, as I have said before, there a small township has sprung
up, which likewise can boast of two boarding-houses. A steamer
calls there regularly from the Bluff, and a magistrate's court
is also held.   In addition there is a school-house.   The
population in and about the township is about 100.

We went to Thompson's boarding-house, and were wel-
comed by the man who had hailed us when we were enjoying
the rain at Maori Beach. His house was a two-storied one,
constructed, of course, of wood, with a number of small bed-
rooms up stairs, plainly but comfortably furnished, and down
stairs a good-sized sitting room, in which was displayed a
well-arranged collection of minerals and curios gathered from
about Stewart Island.   There was also a large, long room,
where the boarders take their meals. A good many visitors
from the mainland stay here in the summer time. At the
time of our visit he had none, and we sat down to dinner with
himself and family.   They had killed a bull that morning, and
we had some of the flesh for dinner. Being served up hot it
was not so very tough, but I knew perfectly well what it would
be like the next time it was placed on the table. After dinner
we had a yarn with Thompson, who shewed us about 1 dwt.

of gold he had recently got from a beach near at hand, and also some pieces of white metal similar to the piece we had found at Horse-shoe Bay.

At about 1.30 p.m. the Captain, the "Squire," "Martha," Peter the Dane, and myself started and walked over to Paterson's Inlet—the distance being about two-and-a-half miles across a ridge about 400 feet high, covered with the usual bush. The track was very good, and the walk extremely pleasant. We arrived at Paterson's Inlet at a little cove called Deep Bay. There we found a whale-boat which we had been told of at Half-Moon Bay—launched the boat, and getting into her pulled over to the Island of Ulva.

Paterson's Inlet is a magnificent sheet of water 15 miles long and from one to six wide. The world's fleet might ride in it at safety. It is dotted with numerous wood-covered islands, and it is enclosed with bush-covered hills, which almost assume the magnitude of mountains at his head, Mount Anglem, the highest peak, attaining an altitude of 3,200 feet. The waters of the inlet teem with fish; rock oysters are numerous on the shore, and bed oysters are dredged up from the deep water. Twelve years ago George Thompson, of Dunedin, and I went to the head of the inlet in a small boat, and, proceeding some miles up a river emptying into the inlet, camped out on a flat—about the only flat clear of bush, I may mention, that is to be found in Stewart Island. Even that is half a swamp, covered with Maori-heads, flax, tussock, rushes, and reeds. Maori-head is the name given to a kind of grass which grows in tufts on stones, often several feet long. It is always found in swampy ground, and when the swamp is drained the Maori-heads disappear. Tussock is a grass common all over New Zealand; it grows in tufts, is wiry and tough like Esparto grass—the stock, especially horses, do very well on it.

Thomson and I stayed some time with a Mr. C. Traill on the Island of Ulva, which he owns. We were at the time on a cruise round Stewart Island in the cutter "Rosa," then owned by Traill's brother, and now at the service of our party. The object of our present visit to Ulva was to call on Mr. Traill. After a stiff pull of about four miles in a strong side breeze and rough water—all of us getting more or less wet— we arrived at a snug little harbour, about 50 yards from Mr. Traill's abode. The latter consists of a comfortable dwelling-house, with store attached, for Mr. Traill sells provisions, oars, ropes, fishing-tackle, hooks, and various other articles needed by the fishing and coasting population of Stewart Island. He is the only honest storekeeper I ever met in the colonies. His articles are what he says they are, and his prices such as I am sure must leave but small profit. I walked up the smooth path from the landing place to the house, thinking of twelve years ago, when Mrs. Traill, a pleasant, intellectual lady, gave us a hearty welcome, and was so untiring in her efforts to promote our comfort that we almost felt ashamed at the trouble and inconvenience to which we were putting her. Now, but a stone's throw from the house, under the spreading branches of a dark-foliaged tree, that lady sleeps in the Lord. She died a few years after our visit, her husband being her only attendant. He had to perform the last sad offices, all that the living and strong can do for the dying and dead, alone, without assistance. Picture a kind, cultured, gentle, Christian gentleman, whom from a position of affluence the waves of adversity had washed to this wilderness, where he had made a comfortable home for his wife and daughter— much helped and cheered in his labours by his living com- panion, helpmate, friend and wife—picture him closing the eyes which could smile on him no more, making the coffin, digging the grave, putting the cold earth on all that remained of her he loved so much, and then resuming his quiet sad life alone. I have been told that he was as one in a maze for long after her death, nor do I wonder.

Mr. Traill is a gentleman of considerable scientific acquire- ments. He was once a flourishing merchant on the mainland; but owing to the rashness of one of his partners his firm failed, and with the wreck of his fortune he retired to Stewart Island, where, taking possession of the Island of Ulva—about five miles round—he opened a store and school, his customers and scholars being composed entirely of Maories. He has made a beautiful garden about his dwelling, and in it roses, hawthorns, apples, pears, plums, cherries, berry bushes, and various rare plants collected from New Zealand, Australia, Herves and Chattam Islands, including several varieties of palms, flourish. His collection, I believe, could only be beaten by that belonging to Sir George Grey in his far-famed Island of Kawau, about 40 miles from Auckland. I found Mr. Traill in his store, tall, thin, bent, and grey; his intellectual

face very worn and weary looking. He remembered me quite
well, and after selling us a few things we required, including
a pair of sculls for the dingy, he asked us to take a walk
through his little kingdom. He has laid out a considerable
extent of land in plantations, shrubberies, &c. First he had
to clear away the native bush, and then, as the soil of Ulva is
too poor, he brought tons and tons of earth from the mainland
of Stewart Island. Besides the trees I have already mentioned, he had a fine collection of rhododendrons, azaleas, and
laburnums, now in bloom. The whole thing does him great
credit. He said that apples, pears, and other fruit ripened
very well.

Stewart Island is in the 48th degree of south latitude, a latitude in most parts of the Southern Ocean liable at any time of
the year to snow, hail, and frost. Stewart Island, however,
enjoys a mild climate, much milder than that of the larger
portion of the South Island—the south, centre, and east coast,
as far as the north boundary of the Province of Canterbury.
In proof of this I may state that Mr. Traill grows semi-
tropical trees and shrubs in the open air, and that it would
be impossible to do in the districts of the South Island I
have mentioned. Snow never lies long, and the frosts on the
low levels are very slight, the thermometer sometimes reaching
freezing point for an hour or two and no more. The reason
of this is the existence of a warm ocean current, which
washes the north-east coast of Australia, and, flowing in a
south-east course, strikes the west coast of New Zealand at
about latitude 42° south somewhere near Hokitika, continues
down the coast, washes round Stewart Island, and then loses
itself in the Southern Ocean. No doubt if this current did not
exist, icebergs from the Antarctic seas would ground on Stewart
Island. They are frequently met with in the Southern Ocean
much nearer the equator. Queensland timber, brought by
this current, is often washed up on the west coast south of
Hokitika ; and about eighteen months ago a Queensland turtle,
three feet long, was caught alive in Mason's Bay, on the west
coast of Stewart Island.

Among the trees Mr. Traill pointed out, was what he called
a " Ti Mi" tree, and which he said was only found growing in
one place in New Zealand, that being Mokaia, on the west
coast of the North Island. He stated that the Maori tradition about it was this—that the first Maories who visited

D

New Zealand came in a large canoe built of "Ti Mi" wood, and they landed at Mokaia, where there is a good harbour. The canoe got broken up, and some of the planks took root and grew. Mr. Traill showed us a fine collection of shells and curios. He informed me that lately the Maories had been getting a good deal of gold, some of it in pieces weighing a couple of dwts. or so, about Paterson's Inlet. As the Maories look upon Mr. Traill as a kind of father, and would certainly take him what gold they got before going to any one else, this statement will be correct. Mr. Traill's daughter, at the time of our trip, was living on the mainland for her education, so that he was all alone.

After a most interesting visit, we bade good-bye to the recluse, and, pulling to sea, I steered my gallant crew from Ulva's dark and lonely isle to Deep Bay. The wind had gone down, the evening was fine and pleasant, and the pull proved to be very enjoyable, the scenery reminding me very much of the English Lakes. We had an enjoyable walk over the hill to Half-Moon Bay, carrying the provisions, &c., that we had bought from Mr. Traill. Most of our party decided to sleep at Thompson's, and after having tea with them—again attacking the bull, this time so tough that one came to the conclusion that he must indeed have been a warrior—I returned to the cutter. Very pretty indeed looked Half-Moon Bay that quiet, calm evening, encircled with undulating bush-covered hills, its numerous white sandy coves and rocky peaks, which latter, projecting from the still water, form picturesque islands scattered about the bay.

The blot on the scenery was the ugly settlers' huts, and the numerous dead, dying, and fallen trees which marked the ravages of that animal—man. I learned from Thompson that he and others have about 3,000 sheep running at the head of Paterson's Inlet, but they do not do very well. They get some 30 per cent. of lambs, but that will barely suffice to keep up their stock, inasmuch as the death rate is a heavy one. Their clip averages about 4½ lb. per sheep, and they get about 9d. a lb. for the wool at the Bluff. They sell most of the mutton eaten on Stewart Island—perhaps about 200 head a-year—which will give them, say £100; add £500 for the wool, and their gross returns will come to about £600 per annum. They pay 25s. a ton freight for the carriage of the wool to the mainland, and 18s. a hundred for shearing their sheep, and rent, perhaps, £40 a-year. It would cost them about £1000 to put the sheep on the run, and if they borrowed the money, interest will be at the rate of 10 per cent., or £100 a-year. So that their total expenses will be £100 + £27 (shearing), + £10 (carriage), + £40 (rent), = £77—say, £200 a-year—which leaves about £400 to divide among them, there being, I believe, three partners in the concern. I have not put down anything for wages, because the partners do the work themselves. This is not much but Thompson is satisfied, and, with what he makes from his accommodation house, is a prosperous man, earning more than he spends year by year. It is a pity that very few people in New Zealand are at present as well off as this Stewart islander.

The next day was wet. I went ashore and had breakfast at Thompson's—the old bull, of course, very tough—and then putting on oilskins we sallied out to spend the day as best we could. Presently we saw coming round a point in the harbour a small dingy with one man in it, who pulled manfully and made good way against a strong wind and considerable sea, his little craft dancing like a cockle shell on the choppy waves. This proved to be the Rev. Mr. Deck, to whom we were introduced. We soon discovered that he and the "Squire" were well acquainted. He was a medium, if anything undersized, wiry, weather-beaten, grey-haired, fussy old gentleman, with a good shaped head and sharp features. He is Justice of the Peace, doctor, and minister for the Island, and had pulled round from a little bay where he lives, about three miles off, to hold a court at the school-house, Half-Moon Bay. He owns a pretty little cutter of about two tons, called the "Foam," which we could see at anchor in the Bay. This he uses to go about to the different settlements of Stewart Island, the crew consisting of himself—captain—wife, mate, and a boy.

Having nothing else to do we attended the court—a wooden building of about 20 feet by 12 feet in extent, with a few plain deal forms in it, a desk and a blackboard. Under the blackboard the Bench, consisting of Mr. Deck and the schoolmaster, a solemn, melancholy-looking individual, took their seats. There were besides ourselves about a dozen lookers-on hanging about the court. The only case was a summons for debt. The defendant was ordered to pay 30s. a month, whereupon plaintiff bluntly said, "that's not enough; he makes £10 a month." "Thirty shillings a month is the order of

.the court," said Mr. Deck. A difficulty then arose about making out the order, the R. M. of the Island having gone away, and taken all the forms with him. While the matter was being discussed, a man put his head inside the door and called out, "the tug's coming, sir." (The tug was the steamer which calls at regular intervals from the mainland, and her arrival is *the* excitement of life at Half-Moon Bay.) In a minute the court was cleared of all but Bench, the policeman and plaintiff. His worship got up and said, "as I want to meet the steamer, I will adjourn the court, and we will settle this matter afterwards." Thereupon the court adjourned, and everybody went to the jetty to meet the steamer.

She was soon alongside—a powerful little boat of about 150 tons. She landed the mails, a few stores, and two or three passengers, one of them being a Dunedin gentleman with whom I have a slight acquaintance. The steamer took some freight on board in the shape of timber and wool, and again steamed away after a stay of about half an hour.

It was now dinner time, and we all repaired to Thompson's, where we found Mr. Deck and his wife, and the Dunedin gentleman and a friend of his, who were going to stay a few days at the establishment. The tough bull was again served up as the *pièce de résistance*, and seemed rather to nonplus the Dunedin men. After dinner newspapers brought by the tug were put upon the table. They were the first papers we had seen since leaving the Bluff, and we read in one of them a flourishing account of the departure of our party to the West Coast in charge of Mr. R. Paulin, C.E.

About 3 p.m. Mr. Deck said to his wife, "it is time we started, Kate; so while you are getting ready, I will go and get my yacht in trim." He then went on board with the boy and got all ready for sailing, returned and fetched his wife, and in a few minutes the "Foam" was gliding out of the harbour.

The heavy rain had been accompanied with a change of wind, which, if it held, would suit us to a T. So we settled up with Thompson, and our party, shouldering their swags, marched down to the beach, and were taken on board the "Rosa," the Dunedin gentleman and others wishing us luck as they shook hands and said "good-bye."

It was the first night we had all slept on board, and four of us found it a tight fit in the cabin, there being only two bunks one could get a stretch in. The Captain went forward, and the

"Squire" took his bunk. I kept my own. "Martha" and "Rameses" made up a shake-down, their heads and shoulders being stowed away somewhere near the rudder case, and the rest of their bodies and limbs supported by the top of the stove, an empty case, and a gun case.

The next morning, the 18th, found it blowing hard from the old quarter, but we determined to try and make Port William at any rate, for that would be so much on our road. So up anchor and away soon after daylight. It blew so furiously though that, with close-reefed sail, it was all we could do to make Horse-shoe Bay, and some of us were not at all sorry when at 11 a.m. we dropped anchor in that snug little harbour, and the men took up their quarters in the hut they had previously occupied.

Thus a fortnight had passed and we were no further forward, and so we decided to supplement our store of provisions. Accordingly, in the afternoon, several others and myself walked over to Thompson's at Half-Moon Bay, got what we wanted, and carried the goods back to Horse-shoe Bay. The night closed in with a heavy south-west gale, barometer 30·02, and very cold.

The 19th was a fine, summer-like day, but what wind there was blew in a wrong direction, and as a heavy sea was running outside, we did not attempt to continue the voyage.

I started the men sinking a shaft; they went down about eight feet, and came on granite in a decomposed state, but found no mineral save a little white metal—native bismuth probably.

CHAPTER V.

THE next morning was what we wanted. Barometer 30·14, weather fine, wind east, and light. So we started, hoping that at last we should get away from stormy Stewart Island. At 8 a.m. we slipped out of Horse-shoe Bay, passed the entrance to Port William, just getting a glimpse of Deaf Dick's house, and shaped our course for Puysegur Point on the mainland.

The day was beautiful, with moderate south-east wind and smooth sea, and we went comfortably along at about five knots an hour. All hands were on deck, lying about yarning, and enjoying the warmth and sunshine and little motion. The wind was so steady that the man at the wheel was the only one who had anything to do. Till noon, by which time we had progressed about 20 miles, we kept close to Stewart Island on the left. A white mist rested on Mount Anglem, said to be the sign of easterly weather. Away to the right and north the Bluff Hill, about 20 miles distant, looked like an island, and in the same direction snow-capped peaks could be seen in any quantity, being the summits of various lofty ranges on the mainland. We could see numerous little white sand coves and bays dotting the Stewart Island coast—some of them at a

distance standing out so distinct against the dark bush as to
have the appearance of sails.

Newton's Beach, about four miles from Port William, is said
to be haunted by Newton's ghost, and the Maories will not go
along it at dark. All I could learn about Newton was that a
man of that name once lived about that part of the world,
fishing, sealing, &c. About 1 p.m. we were nearly clear of
Stewart Island, and began to feel the heave of the Southern
Ocean.

As we left Stewart Island we passed close to Raggedty Point,
the most north-west point of the Island, and from which our
course to Puysegur Point was about west-north-west magnetic.

Raggedty Point is about the roughest piece of coast scenery
I have seen for some time. Here a series of granite needles
rise from the sea for a distance of several miles; one might
fancy it the sunken jaw of some huge monster, with the sharp-
pointed teeth projecting above the ocean. At 4 p.m., as we
cleared Stewart Island, the swell from south grew heavier—a
long, regular, rolling swell, so big as to prevent all view when
we were in its trough. No other land than Stewart Island was
now in sight, as a mist to the north shut out the mainland.
The breeze kept steady, and our little craft went on bravely,
climbing up and sliding down the huge green rollers, and at
4 p.m. we were within 24 miles of Puysegur Point, and could
see the mountains of the mainland looming in the distance.
Stewart Island looked like a fog bank on the horizon behind us,
being nearly 40 miles off. Nearly due south and about 12
miles distant, the Solander Islands showed clear and distinct.
These islands are two isolated masses of rock, several hundred
feet high (the largest one, I was told, was 600ft.), bearing
south 24½ east, 30 miles from Puysegur Point. There is a
lighthouse on one of them. A New Zealand Government
steamer calls once every three months with provisions, &c.
and they are occasionally visited by parties of seal hunters.

The wind began to get light and shew signs of shifting as
evening came on, and we commenced to get a bit anxious lest
we should not weather the point before it shifted; for, had it
come on to blow from the west, we should have had to run
again for Stewart Island or the Bluff.

At 6 p.m. we were about 12 miles off the mainland, and could
see the coast very well. A most uninviting one it looked, with
its iron-bound rocks and huge mountain masses rising imme-

diately behind, clothed with dark, thick bush for about 2,000
or 3,000 feet, and snow-covered peaks above that rising to
over 6,000 feet above sea level.

These form part of the Billow and Princess Mountain ranges,
in the vicinity of Lake Hauroto, which lake was explored and
surveyed—at least the upper portion of it—by George and
James Thompson and myself in 1882.

As the sun set the wind got lighter and lighter, heavy clouds
and masses of white mist rested on and hung about the mountains, occasional showers of rain fell, and the southerly swell
was getting heavier.   I had several times before been in this
part of the world in different steamers, and always found it
raining or snowing.

At nightfall we were beclamed about 12 miles from Puysegur
Point and four off the coast, with a tremendous swell from the
south setting us on shore, and our prospects looked a little
glum.

Patsey, the sailor, enlivened us with some tales.   I would
back him against most for pitching a yarn.   One was—that
once he and another spent some weeks on the large Solander
Island, and finding time hang heavy on their hands they
amused themselves by sliding from the top of the highest peak
to the bottom on a piece of seaweed.

From the base to the summit of this peak is a vein of rock
which, seen from the cutter, looked smooth and shiny as though
it had been polished by friction.   I noticed this while Patsey
was telling his yarn, and when he had finished I pointed to it
and said, " I quite believe you.   I can see where you and
your seaweed have worn the rocks smooth, even from here."
Whereat there was a laugh, and as similar veins of rock were
afterwards observed about the sounds, they got the name of
Patsey's slides.

Another yarn ran thus: A man named Price once went to
the Solanders, meaning to help himself to a lot of seal skins
which he knew the Maories had stored there.   Price thought
the Maories were away, and not likely to come back for some
time, but unfortunately for him, while he was helping himself,
the Maories returned and caught him.   They smashed his
boat, took all the provisions and skins there were on the island,
including his, and left him to get on as best he could.   But
Price was equal to the occasion.   He killed some seals, which
furnished him with food, and, making a raft of the skins, sailed

to Price's Harbour on the mainland, where there is a Maori settlement. Here he found a goodly store of seal skins, and the Maories all away. Price was in luck this time. He took all the skins and got clear away with them before the Maories returned.

As night drew on apace we crept nearer and nearer to the shore, looking in vain for Puysegur lighthouse light, which Patsey, who was supposed to know the coast, said we were bound to see until within a mile from the coast, when the land would shut it in. The Captain, although he had not been there before, did not think from the appearance of the coast, as shewn by the chart, that this was the case; and it turned out afterwards that we needed to have been at least six miles from the coast to have seen the light.

At midnight we were not more than a mile-and-a-half from the shore, every roller giving us a lift nearer. The sea was like glass, but the swell was tremendous, and its thunder as it broke upon the rocks too loud to be pleasant. The cutter would not answer her helm. We had the spanker set, and it swept the deck from side to side as the cutter rolled and jumped about in the swell.

All our party, myself excepted, were below, more or less sick, one of them having a bucket fixed up in his bunk. I was most of the time on deck discussing the situation with the Captain, and we occasionally went below to consult the chart. Though put out a bit at not seeing Puysegur light which, according to Patsey, we ought to have seen from where we supposed ourselves to be, the Captain had, as we found afterwards, a correct notion of our position, and expressed his opinion rather forcibly as to Patsey's information, inasmuch as relying upon it, he had come nearer the shore than he meant to do.

We were off one of the most treacherous parts of the New Zealand coast, where it is never long without a gale or squall, and always swept by strong and varying currents.

Not long ago a cutter was caught just where we were becalmed, washed ashore by the swell, and ground to pieces in a few minutes. It was not a cheerful look out, and one of the sailors was in a funk. "Oh! Lord, isn't that awful," he kept on saying, as the breakers sounded louder and louder. However, shortly after 1 a.m. a squall came up from the west, and the " Rosa " was soon pushing along, with her stern to the shore and her nose nearly due south-half-west, as if she meant business. It did not last long, but when it died out we were out of danger from the surf and in a position to round Puysegur Point should a blow from the south-west, of which there were strong indications, come on.

The south-wester did come up at daylight, but only a fresh breeze, and when the sun rose we were bowling along with a fair wind almost round the wished for point.

Some dangerous-looking rocks off the mainland to the north-west, about eight miles off, were pointed out as being Green Islets boat harbour, where there is good shelter for boats. From Puysegur Point, 10 miles west, to beyond the mouth of the Waiau, 45 miles to the east of Green Islets, gold has been found, sometimes in considerable quantities, along the beach and at the mouth of the rivers by different parties of adventurous explorers.

The inaccessibility of the country and difficulty of obtaining provisions has hitherto prevented more than short visits being made to it, a few men going with a month or two's provisions, and having to return as soon as their provisions were exhausted.

I am of opinion that some day a considerable gold field will be opened up in this district. I form this belief from what men who have been there have told me, and from specimens of gold brought by them.

A few weeks before we left the Bluff a party with provisions for several months had started from the same port in a large whale-boat. There were, I believe, five men, and they proceeded to Green Islets, and there landed, intending to spend some months prospecting. We could see no sign of them, and wondered if they could see us, as we heard afterwards they did, and were watching our movements with the utmost anxiety. They tried unsuccessfully to attract our attention, for they had met with disaster. They had not properly secured their boat, and, leaving her too far down the beach, a violent storm smashed her to pieces, with the result that they were left with very little provisions and no means of getting away. Seeing we kept on our course they hoped we were going into Preservation Inlet, and, starting off, made their way with great difficulty over a very rough country to the Inlet—a distance in a straight line of about 12 miles—only to find we were not there. They then made their way to the lighthouse and got provided for, until a vessel calling there took them home.

At 8 a.m. we were just abreast of the lighthouse placed on Puysegur Point, and soon got our first view of a West Coast sound, as we opened up the entrance of the most southerly of them named Preservation Inlet.

I can well imagine the mariner who named this sound after fighting his way through one of the storms so common in these seas, perhaps being nearly lost on the harbourless coast we had just passed, and at last, finding himself in the perfect shelter of the sound, naming it from the bottom of his heart " Preservation Inlet." We had a good view up the sound as we sailed across its entrance, which extends from Puyseger Point on the south to Gulche's Head on the north, a distance of about five miles.

The sound or inlet extends inland about 20 miles, having various smaller arms branching from the main one, which is called Long Sound. There are numerous islands about the entrance, the largest of which—Coal Island—contains about 2,500 acres. It is so named from coal having been found on it, but not as yet in any quantities. For about seven miles up the sound is about five miles wide. After that, to its head, it varies between one and two miles in width. The coastline is picturesque and varied in the extreme. Both the main inlet and its branches are hemmed in by steep mountains, covered with dense forest, which almost everywhere take their rise very abruptly from the water's edge, their peaks averaging close on 4000 feet, some of them being more, and the forest extending 3000 feet up their sides. The streams flowing from them into the inlet are all more or less cascades and torrents.

Soundings taken about this inlet shew a depth of from 15 to 20 fathoms across the entrance and for two miles inward; beyond that to within a mile or two of the head about 50 fathoms is the general depth, as much as 90 being met with in the vicinity of Coal Island. The waters teem with fish, and the air with sand-flies. This sound has, perhaps, had more explorers in it than any of the others. A little gold has been found and a few thin seams of coal. We did not go up the sound, but could see a good deal of it as we sailed across its mouth.

A broken mountainous peninsula with peaks over 4,000 feet high, 15 miles long and 5 wide at its greatest width, and connected with the mainland by a hilly ridge about 2,000 yards across, separates Preservation Inlet from Chalky or Dark Inlet. The mouth of Chalky Inlet extends from Gulche's

Head to Cape Providence, a distance of about seven miles. A large island of chalk, called Chalky Island, lies right in the centre of the entrance to the inlet. Close to the north of it is another island called Passage Island, a 20-fathom channel intervening. This channel is about half-a-mile wide. At about 10 miles from the entrance the sound divides into two branches, one called Canaris Sound, and another to the north of it called Edwardson's Sound; Canaris being about five and Edwardson's seven miles in length. The shores of this sound and its branches are not so indented as those of Preservation Inlet. It is much broader and very deep at the entrance. Between Gulche's Head and Cape Providence the depth averages about 20 fathoms, and that increases on proceeding up the inlet. Inside Chalky Island, almost up to the head of the water, the depths vary from 50 to 150 fathoms. We passed close to Chalky Island, its white stratified cliffs having a fine appearance, and, with a fresh fair breeze and big following swell, were soon round Cape Providence and running up to Dusky Sound.

The panorama as we sailed past Preservation and Chalky Inlets was very fine. The deep blue inlets penetrating the gloomy, wall-like mountains, snow peaks in the distance, the white mass of Chalky Island in the foreground, and the bright sunshine sparkling on the rippling waters around about us— all combined to produce a grand, pleasing, and most enjoyable picture, across which we glided in comfort and delight.

All on board were on deck and well, save M. and the " Squire," the latter still being in his bunk with a bucket. The Captain, who had been on deck until we were safe round Puysegur Point, a stretch of twenty-four hours, was also now having a sleep in the forehold. Tom, the Dane, was at the helm ; the rest, mostly sitting or lying, were scattered over the deck, chatting about the scenery and discussing last night's experiences. Patsey, too, occasionally came in with some of his yarns, at which everyone laughed and no one believed. A year previously he and three others had, he said, gone to the West Coast in a whale-boat, landed on a beach near Milford Sound, and got 85 ozs. of gold in a couple of months. Then they had a row and separated, Patsey and one man sticking to the boat and making their way down to the Bluff, where their gold did not trouble them long. Poor, improvident Patsey is at present carrying about all his worldly possessions on his back. The other two men made their way over to Martin's Bay Settlement. Patsey disposed of the boat to the party we have already mentioned. They took it to Green Islets, where it was smashed to pieces.

This was Sunday morning, and I went below for a bit, and read the 119th Psalm from my wife's Bible. As I read, I suppose I must have dozed off, for I distinctly seemed to hear the sound of an organ and the voices of a congregation repeating alternate verses; yet, at the same time, I knew I was sitting rather uncomfortable and cold in the old, damp, dark, small, not very clean cabin of the " Rosa," as she drove along over a heavy following swell off Preservation Inlet—sitting on the starboard side, while the "Squire," past speech, lay on the bunk opposite me.

The appearance presented from the sea by the sound district so far seemed this—the land seems at first to rise at a uniform grade, then comes a valley, and then abrupt mountains. At 2 p.m. we were entering Dusky Sound, the water getting smoother every minute, and the scenery superb and improving as we advanced from the sea.

Dusky Sound has one long arm running due east for nearly twenty-five miles. This arm is about three miles wide for nearly the whole length. It is nearly divided into two by a series of islands, which are almost continuous, the two largest being called Long Island and Cooper Island. Long Island is about seven miles long and one across, while Cooper Island has a length of some five miles and a width of about two.

These Islands extend up the middle of the sound from the sea to its head. They are mountainous, forest-clad, and extremely picturesque. At a point about ten miles from the head of this arm, another arm branches off, and extends nearly due north for about twelve miles, when it enters Breaksea Sound; while about half way up it yet another inlet, called Wet-Jacket Arm, branches to the east for a distance of seven miles. The arm connecting Dusky Sound with Breaksea Sound makes the land to the west of it an island. This island is called Resolution Island, and is about 10 miles by seven in extent, besides having attached to its north-west corner a long, narrow peninsula, nine miles long and two wide, extending in a south-westerly direction. This peninsula goes by the name of Five Fingers, and the basin between it and the mainland of Resolution Island is called Five-fingered Inlet.

The entrance to Dusky Sound is about five miles across, extending from South Point on the mainland to Five-fingered Point on Resolution Island. It is studded with islands, the largest of which—Anchor Island—is about four miles by one, forest clad, and having hills between one and two thousand feet in altitude. There is also a small lake on this island.

We sailed round the west of Anchor Island, and proceeded up Five-fingered Inlet, keeping about half-a-mile off the shore of Five-fingered Peninsula, our destination being Cormorant Cove, a little bay on the mainland of Resolution Island near the head of the Inlet.

Very beautiful was that Sunday afternoon, as with our sails stretched before the breeze which followed us in from the sea, we sped over the blue waters of the inlet, the swell getting less and less till it became imperceptible. Numerous penguins were seen standing on the rocks which everywhere lined the shore, and heard calling with harsh notes from numerous caves and holes. Gulls, ducks, cormorants and divers were flying and swimming about in all directions. To the left rose the forest-clad heights of Five-finger Peninsula; in front of us mountainous Resolution Island, some of its peaks reaching 4,000 feet, towered majestically out of the waters; while to the right and behind us stretched an ocean studded with picturesque, hilly, wood-covered islands and rocky peaks. Behind all stood out in bold relief a range of huge bush-clad mountains, many of the higher peaks clothed in a mantle of eternal snow.

Over the deep blue water just rippled by the breeze, past fairy-like, rocky, and densely-wooded islands, under the shadow, as it were, of overhanging and magnificently-timbered mountains, we bowled along, and at 4 p.m. dropped anchor in Cormorant Cove in about 10 fathoms of water. It was a truly beautiful spot, completely shut in by lofty hills with mountains behind them. Many cataracts could be seen and more heard, those in the distance having the appearance of silver streaks tumbling over steep rocks and winding through the dark forest. The sound of falling waters blended pleasantly with the trilling of the land songsters and the harsher notes of the feathered denizens of the deep.

CHAPTER VI.

THE soundings between South and Five-fingered Points
run between 50 and 60 fathoms, and in Five-fingered
Inlet between 20 and 70. Up the main arm they average about
55 fathoms, but for three or four miles off the south of Resolution Island depths of from 100 to 162 fathoms are met with.
Up the North Arm they vary between 50 and 100, and in
Wet-Jacket Arm from 27 to 112.

It being a fine evening, as soon as the anchor was down and
the sails furled, both the whale-boat and dingy were lowered
and the cutter deserted. I went in the whale-boat with most
of our party, and pulled about three miles to the head of the
cove, where we found a torrent pouring into the cove through
a steep gorge.

The scenery here beggars description; it must be seen to be
properly appreciated. The wind had died away, and the water
into which we dipped our oars was like a sheet of glass;
and the beautiful picture formed by forest-clad mountains and
islands, cascades and rocky, snow-flecked, sun-gilded peaks
was mirrored with a softer, even more bewitching beauty in
the still surface of the deep. Stately black swans, many of
them with cygnets, ducks, teal, divers, and gulls were gliding
about or floating, shadow-haunted, on the blue waters; while

on shore colonies of penguins sat bolt upright among the rocks and roots of trees near to the water's edge, calling to each other, and seeming to screech defiance to the intruders. About half-a-mile away I see the Captain and his men approaching a group of swans. Puff, bang! and a loud report goes echoing over the still waters and away up the mountain sides, followed by a tremendous splashing of birds' wings, as, in all directions, the feathered denizens of this majestic and usually silent region rise from the water, filling the air with their notes of alarm. The heavy black swans strike the water violently two or three times, and then getting into motion, sail not ungracefully away—all save one, whose wing is broken, and who is soon rowed down and secured by the Captain. We go slowly along, keeping close to the shore, and find a swan's nest containing four fresh eggs. This pleases the " Squire " greatly, and he loses no time in appropriating them. He blew two for his collection, a step some of us rather regretted afterwards, when we found the remaining eggs to be remarkably good eating. We see several fish swimming about, some of them being groper, or hapuka as the Maories call them. They are a voracious, coarse-fleshed fish, sometimes weighing close on 100 lbs. They do not resemble any English fish of which I am aware. They are something like cod, but deeper from the belly to the back, in proportion to their length, and not nearly so good eating. Their flesh is white, very firm and insipid. Groper cutlets (the best way of cooking them) are tolerable with good sauce when one is hungry and has not tasted fish for some time.

It was sunset as we rowed back to the cutter, the last rays of the sun tinting the sky and lofty peaks of the mountains that enveloped us with glorious colours. The gorgeous scenery around us was perfectly reflected in those clear blue depths, and as our oars dipped and we sped onward we seemed to glide over the polished surface of some marvellous painting. It was getting dusk when we got on board, and as the light of a beautiful sunset died away, bright stars shone over the dark mountains from out Heaven's unclouded canopy. The screech of the kakapo (big ground parrot) and the penguin, the whistle of the kiwi (wingless night bird) and the kaka, the wailing weird cry of the weka (Maori or wood hen), and the hushed murmur of many waterfalls all mingled in a delightful musical babel which was in full chorus when we turned into our bunks. And so ended our first day in the Sounds of New Zealand.

The 22nd was a very fine morning, with a cloudless sky and no wind, and, again manning the two boats, all hands left the cutter at 7 a.m., and proceeded to the head of the Five-fingered Inlet. We in the whale-boat easily rowed away from the dingy. We had Jack, the big retreiver, with us, and also little Fan, who had taken a fancy to me and would follow no one else.

The weather was glorious and the superb scenery, the temperature being between 60° and 70°. The hot, bright sunlight made everything cheerful. The water was like a mirror, reflecting the bright sky and lofty hills and mountains to perfection, its surface dotted as on the previous day with black swans, gulls, ducks, cormorants, penguins, and divers. We were soon out of sight of the cutter, and, emerging from the snug little cove, proceeded up the inlet—here about two miles wide and distant four miles from the head. A slight swell from the sea was perceptible, and could be seen breaking on the shore of Five-fingered Peninsula.

When we were yet three miles from the head and about one from the nearest point on shore, one of our party aimed a gun at a bird, whereupon Jack the dog, who has a mortal dread of guns, sprang overboard and made for land. It was useless calling him back and I declined to go after him, as I knew, from what I had seen of his swimming powers, he would make the land easily enough. So we pulled on, and soon could only just make out the ripple caused by Master Jack as he made for a point about three miles below our destination.

As we progressed, the mountains on either side assumed the appearance of cliffs which had been rent asunder, leaving a rift between them about a mile wide; the sea flowing through this rift transformed Five-fingered Peninsula into an island. In the middle of the rift is an accumulation of sand and timber, raised a few feet above high water mark, about half-a-mile across, and joining the Peninsula to Resolution Island. About two miles from the head we began to see the bottom, and at about a mile found ourselves in shallow water, passing over a mud flat strewn with sunken snags. As it was high water, we concluded that at low water the flat would be bare. We found the head of the inlet low and swampy, and we had to wade from our boat to firm ground. This flat is covered with low

E

bush, flax and Maori heads, and having secured the boat, we started to make our way across to Hen Cove, being well provided with picks, shovels, axes, slashers, and prospecting dishes.   The slashers are like small bill-hooks on one side and a chopper on the other, and are very useful for cutting through the dense undergrowth of creepers, vines, and ferns so common in the New Zealand bush, especially on the West Coast.   We made our way through the scrub for about half-a-mile, and then arrived at the head of Hen Cove.

Hen Cove is a small inlet from the sea about two miles long and three-quarters wide. It has evidently been joined to Five-fingered Inlet, the passage having been blocked by the accumulation of drift forming the flat we had just crossed. Emerging from the bush, we found ourselves on an enormous pile of drift timber—some of it wreckage—extending right across the head of the cove, and about 50 yards deep.   The sea comes close up to it at high water, and, I have no doubt, washes among it during storms.   Scrambling across this drift we got on firm, hard sand, which, however, did not extend down either side of the cove.   At low water there is about a quarter of a mile of sand, bare at the head, but below that, on each side, the mountains descend almost precipitously into the sea.

Everyone was soon busy with pick and shovel, some going one side of the cove and some the other, sinking holes, scraping rocks, and washing out stuff in the dishes.   As far as I could see, a uniform granite formation everywhere prevailed ; but where the surface is so covered with carpets of forest, bush, and fern, it is difficult to form an opinion of what the formation really is.   There were no signs of slates or schist.   There were, however, a few small fragments of marble, and numerous veins of quartz and quartz fragments about the rocks. We did not find a trace of gold, but came across one small piece of galena, and large quantities of what I believe to be almandite, a variety of garnet composed of silicate of aluminium and iron.   Most of it had a brownish red appearance, rather opaque ; but a little was fine transparent red, having almost the appearance of precious garnet.   We also found much mica, and a good deal of iron pyrites.

At about 5 p.m. we knocked off work, and returned to the head of Five-fingered Inlet.   The tide was out, and a good mile of soft mud intervened between our boats and the water, save for a little creek which coursed in a zig-zag direction down the middle of the flat, and which, 400 yards away, was deep enough to float the dingy. We also found Jack the dog asleep in the whale-boat. He must have had a hard scramble from where he landed to have reached the boat, and, indeed, seemed quite knocked up.

The Captain, "Martha," M., "Rameses" and myself carried the dingy over the mud for 400 yards, till the creek was deep enough to float her. We went up to our ankles in the yielding mud at almost every step we took, and often deeper. Having accomplished our task, "Rameses" and I returned to the whale-boat to wait for the turn of the tide. The occupants of the dingy, however, started on their return journey to the cutter.

It was now about 5.30 p.m., and as there was no chance of the whale-boat being afloat before 7 p.m., I made my way back to Hen Cove, the sand-flies annoying us terribly about the boat, where the Danes were washing. These insect pests, however, proved to be quite as troublesome at the cove, where Patsey and Tom the sailor had remained. Tom was trying to shoot Maori hens, while Patsey made a fire and tried to snare some, which would have been welcome, for we had eaten nothing since morning. Although there were any quantity of both black and brown ones hopping about the piled-up drift wood, all our efforts to catch them failed, so we gave up trying, and smoked and yarned by the fire, standing in as much of the smoke as we could bear to keep off the clouds of sand-flies. Presently we were joined by the "Squire," who had been for some hours away looking for something to kill with his walking-stick gun. He had not had much success.

We were much amused watching Tom the sailor, who, with an old fowling piece, was blazing away at everything without any material result. I do not think there was a mortality of 20 per cent. from his discharges. He was doing his best to shoot a Maori hen, of which there were numbers pecking about the drift timber. They would let him get to within a few feet of them, for they are very tame, especially in out-of-the-way places. I have thrown stones at them and hit them, and even then they would only run a few steps and come back again. We saw Tom crawl to within a few feet of one, take aim and fire. The hen looked at him, and quietly moved a step or two further along the dead log she was on. Tom loads, gets into position a little nearer than before, and fires again. The hen, unhurt, walks slowly away, and disappears among the drift timber. Tom gave it up and came back to the fire. He laughed at his non-success, and said that a hen was looking down the barrel once when he fired, and yet he missed her.

We stayed by the fire till nearly 7 o'clock, the "Squire" wearing a coloured handkerchief round his head to keep the flies off. We then returned to the whale-boat, and the tide being in, started off for our floating home. I steered, and we had a most enjoyable row to the cutter, for it was another glorious, calm evening, and swans, grey, blue and paradise ducks, cormorants, gulls, divers, &c., were disporting themselves on the glassy water, made like a sea of molten gold by the reflection of the setting sun. As we got down the inlet and crossed over to Cormorant Cove, there was a gentle swell from the far-off ocean which could be felt and no more, and just heard as it broke in murmuring wavelets on the rocks of Five-fingered Peninsula. Numerous penguins lined the shore close to the water's edge, and their harsh notes were to be heard at intervals breaking on the silence of the night. It was dusk when we reached the cutter a little tired and very hungry.

The 23rd was calm, clear, hot. We weighed anchor at 8 a.m., and rowed the cutter out of romantic Cormorant Cove. Lovely it is, with a beauty that surpasses even the scenery at the head of Ulswater. The water here was only half salt, a fact to be accounted for by the numerous cataracts and torrents pouring in from the surrounding mountains. We always found this to be the case at or near the heads of the inlets. In some instances the water was quite fresh, and there was always a downward current perceptible. Slowly we drew out of the cove, and headed down the inlet.

Beautiful and enchanting, indeed, was the last view we had of the cove—the little harbour smooth as a mill-pond, a blue sapphire gem resting at the base of a stupendous emerald casket. The bush on the hills and mountains consisted chiefly of birch, with a good sprinkling of pines (chiefly the handsome-foliaged remu or red pine), iron-wood, kewai, and tree-ferns, with the usual undergrowth of ferns, supple-jacks, moss, and vines. The birch, the chief timber of the West Coast as far as quantity goes, is a very fine tree. There are several varieties of it—namely, the red, black, and white birch. Of these, the black is the best timber. Seen from a distance, they all have much the same appearance. The foliage is a small, round leaf, with a bright lustre, which, when the sunlight catches it, has a very pleasing effect.

The bush teems with feathered songsters—notably the tui, bell-bird and robin. The robin, I think, may be called the most accomplished singer, for the other birds, though very musical, possess far fewer notes, and do not sustain their efforts at melody nearly so long as the robin. The tui is about as big as the blackbird, quite black, with projecting white feathers under its throat, which gives it the appearance of wearing a tie. It is sometimes called the parson bird on that account. The robin is just like an English robin, only that it has a brownish-black body and white breast. The bell-bird has a most musical bell-like note; it is a little smaller than a thrush, with a longish beak. Small yellow canaries were numerous; they are sometimes to be seen in large flocks, chattering like sparrows. This is always considered a sure sign of rain. Native crows were also numerous; they are more like magpies than crows in shape, are black in colour, about as big as a moorhen, and have long legs and yellow wattles. They do not fly, but hop to a great distance.

We made but slow progress down the inlet. For one thing we had no proper sweeps, and were compelled to fall back upon the whale-boat oars—a poor substitute. About 10 a.m. the water began to be ruffled with catspaws, and accordingly we took in the oars and drifted along with all sail set. We thought at one time we were in for a fine breeze, but it never once got beyond the light puff stage. Sometimes our sails would fill, and we would hear the welcome ripple as the cutter began to move; but it soon ceased, and we would again be becalmed.

However, the marvellous beauty of the scenery made me, for one, quite reconciled to our slow progress. We were stealing through the most beautiful archipelago imaginable. The deep blue water was studded with islands and islets too numerous to count—all of them rocky, forest-clad and picturesque in the extreme; many of them mountainous, and varying in size from three miles across to rocks just projecting above the water. The whole picture, except between south-west and north-west, was set in a frame of majestic mountains covered with luxuriant foliage, and capped with snow-covered peaks, and, above all, the bluest of skies imaginable. We passed between Pigeon and Parrot Islands, and then between Anchor and Resolution Islands, and eventually found ourselves in the main arm of the sound.

Parrot and Pigeon Islands are both lofty and clothed with forest growth. The former contains about 300 and the latter 600 acres. Anchor Island is about four miles long and half-a-mile wide, its highest point being about 1,400 feet above sea level. There is also a lake about three-quarters of a mile long in the centre of the island.

I may here mention that yesterday, returning to the cutter from the head of the inlet, the party in the dingy saw the ruins of a hut in the bush, some distance from the water. They landed and inspected it. In it they found 60 lbs. of beeswax, a bible, dictionary, a book on surveying, logs, mathematical instruments, stuffed birds and skins, glass eyes, tea and flour, all save the eyes much damaged by the weather and rats. This hut is supposed to have been occupied by a man named Wheeler, who went about collecting bird's skins. He disappeared, and all efforts to trace him failed; it is commonly supposed he met an untimely end. They brought away the instruments, wax, and glass eyes, and I wished they had brought the books, but did not hear of it till it was too late.

It was now 1 p.m. Hitherto the day had been almost calm and the sun so hot that the pitch on deck melted in the seams; but just as we emerged into the main arm we encountered a breeze from the sea so strong that we had to reef sails, and then scudding along at a merry pace for about three miles, finally entered a snug little harbour, called Duck Cove, on the south coast of Resolution Island.

When fairly into the cove it was quite calm. We could see the waters of the main arm we had just left lashed white with the wind, while we had hardly enough to take us to our anchorage. Our progress was rather jerky, for at one time we would be quite becalmed and almost stop; then a puff of wind would come whirling down the mountain side, filling our sails with a bang, and off we would start. The puff would be over in a minute, and then we would gradually come almost to a standstill until another puff started us off again. We proceeded in this fashion for about two miles, and at 2 p.m. came to an anchorage at the head of the cove, opposite to, and about 200 yards from the mouth of a small river.

CHAPTER VII.

BOATS were at once lowered, and all hands went ashore.
The Danes started washing and baking, the baking being
done in what is called a camp oven, a circular iron vessel,
about 6 inches deep, and sometimes 14 across, provided with
a close-fitting lid and a loose handle attached to the oven.
We generally baked by hanging the oven over the fire by the
handle, and covering the lid with hot ashes. The rest of us
went prospecting.

Duck Cove is an indentation on the south of Resolution
Island, extending about two-and-a-half miles. It at one time
evidently extended much further, but the *débris* brought down
from the surrounding mountains has filled the upper portion of
it. This filling-up process is going on in all the sounds. At
their heads are level, swampy flats, evidently deposited by
floods; and I saw on several occasions what had been islands,
now joined to other islands and the mainland by level alluvial
deposits. The river which flows into the head of Duck Cove
rises in the heart of Resolution Island, and is about six miles
long. Its whole course is between steep forest-clad mountains,
from 3,000 to 4,000 feet high. In ascending this river we
found its bed to be composed of hard mountain gneiss, impreg-

nated with hornblende and garnet and numerous quartz veirs, some of the latter shewing a little galena.   We landed near the mouth of the river, and found ourselves on a level alluvial deposit composed of sand, peat, boulders, and timber.   This deposit had filled up the gorge, here about three-quarters of a mile wide, and extending inland some two or three miles.   It is covered with timber and bush, and a dense undergrowth of ferns and creepers.   This undergrowth, intermixed as it was with large quantities of fallen and decayed timber, made progress through it very slow ; the explorer having, in fact, to carve his way with the help of his slasher.   The timber was much the same as previously described, with large quantities of tutu (pronounced tute), and fuchsia.

The tutu, a poisonous bush, is common all over New Zealand.   It has strong light stems, generally about eight feet high, sometimes much less, but on the West Coast much more, 20 and 30 feet being met with.   The berries, which grow in clusters, are reddish brown in colour, juicy, and have a tempting appearance when ripe.   Cattle, horses, and sheep are sometimes killed by eating the shoots, going mad, and dying in convulsions.   However, stock brought up among tutu do not seem to be injured by it.   I know many places in New Zealand where there is any quantity of tutu, and yet the stock feeding about get no harm from the plant.   There have been several cases of children being poisoned through eating the berries, yet, if the berries are put in a piece of muslin and sucked, no harm will result.

The fuchsia is everywhere to be found in New Zealand, wherever, in fact, there is any bush.   It grows to the proportions of a respectably sized tree.   I have seen fuchsia trunks two feet in diameter.   It has a light brown fibrous bark, which is constantly being shed in large strips, giving the trunk and branches of the tree a ragged appearance.   I have an idea this bark might be utilised for commerce.   The flower has green calyx and pinkish green petals.   The berries are about an inch long, in shape like a date stone, soft, pulpy, and juicy, of a reddish brown colour when ripe ; rather nice, and said to be harmless. I, however, doubt if they are, at least if eaten in large quantities, inasmuch as one hot day in summer, when I was making a survey and superintending the cutting of a line through the bush along a hillside, both my assistant and myself got very thirsty, and being unable to find any water and there being plenty of fuchsia trees about with ripe berries on, we ate a considerable quantity. That same evening and part of the next day we both felt a heavy sensation in the head, accompanied with slight fever, caused, I have not the slightest doubt, by our partaking of the berries.

M. told me the following story about the tutu:—Once an elephant belonging to a menagerie camped near the Waitake River, in Canterbury, was turned out in a paddock by the river side to amuse himself. There were numerous clumps of tutu about, and the elephant tore up large armfuls with his trunk and devoured them. Someone saw what he was at, and went and told the proprietor, warning him of the danger to which the elephant was exposed. The proprietor rushed out to bring him away, but it was too late. When he approached the animal the poison had already commenced to work, and the gigantic beast, lifting his trunk, let off a series of terrific trumpet-blasts. Next, he began to dance and spin round in a marvellous manner, and, finally, he charged into the river, where, after lashing the water furiously and trumpeting for a few minutes, he spun round again several times and dropped dead.

Our prospecting was carried on, as usual, with pick, shovel, and dish. We found no gold, but large masses of what "Dana," in his "Text-book of Mineralogy," calls "Avanturine Quartz," spangled with scales of mica. We also discovered a few pieces of white quartz, with small specs of very soft malleable white metal.

We returned to the cutter at sunset. Our Danes had once more proved their utter ignorance of the most elementary knowledge of baking by producing a dreadful, solid, damp substance, in the preparation of which they had consumed an enormous amount of flour. Such as it was, we ate it, making our evening meal off it and tinned meat, which we washed down with some excellent tea.

As the day passed away, we had from the deck of our little cutter a magnificent, romantic panorama. To the north and looking up the cove we saw a deep gorge between steep, wall-like mountains, clothed with dense bush and forest, and looking almost black in the evening light. At the head of the gorge rose several peaks, more than 4,000 feet above the sea level, and for 2,000 feet above the bush line covered with yellow tussock grass. The rays of the setting sun falling on these yellow, grass-encumbered peaks, made them look like burnished copper, and they stood out in extraordinary contrast to the dark, sombre depths of the gorge below. Forest-clad, massive mountains, rising to the height of about 3,000 feet, with a quarter of a mile of water intervening, barred further view to the east and west. To the south, gazing down the cove, was a glimpse of the main sound, here about two-and-a-quarter miles broad.

There was a gale blowing up the sound, and its waters could be seen, dark and angry-looking, flecked with foam from the cresting waves. Then came the wooded hills of Long Island, and, towering above and beyond, the mighty mountain masses of the mainland, their peaks attaining in places an elevation of 6,000 feet, but utterly devoid of vegetation above the bush line—3,000 feet. These peaks appeared to be hard granite rock, with quartz veins showing here and there. On the face of one of these mountains was a mass of white material shaped like a mare's tail. It seemed to break out from the mountain-side about 2,000 feet above sea level, and then to flow for several hundred feet down through the bush without vegetation of any kind on its surface. From the distance it looked not unlike a huge cataract. Some said it was water, but the glass showed it to be a fixed body; it was, perhaps, mud, maybe, decomposed quartz or felspar. We could hear the waves breaking in the open sound and the wind roaring round the mountain sides; but save for an occasional gust, which made our little craft sway at her anchor and which passed as quickly as it came, and for a slight swell, which we scarcely felt but could hear surging on the beach close to us, we were perfectly still. The night turned very dark, so that the faintest outline of the mountains could not now be distinguished; but through the darkness occasionally came the call of the wood hen and the kiwi.

Dusky Sound has, from time to time, during the last hundred years and more, been a harbour of refuge for whalers and storm-tossed mariners. Captain Cook stayed here some time, and grew vegetables for his crew with the object of curing them of scurvy, which, at the time, was making ravages amongst them. Evidences of the bush having been cleared can still be traced in places, and these clearances are said to have been made by the great navigator. He reports that some of his men, when staying here, saw a long, low-bodied, brown-coloured animal with a bushy tail, in the bush; it is generally supposed to have been an error on the part of Cook. Recently, however, Bishop Neville, of Dunedin, gave an account of a long-backed, bushy-tailed animal seen near one of the inland lakes, and two men assert that they shot an animal like an otter on Lake Hauroto. Another individual, I hear, reported seeing a long-backed, thick-tailed animal by the side of the Pyke River, near Big Bay in 1886; and, a year later, I myself saw clear tracks of an animal in the sand, by one of the tributaries of the Pyke, which were certainly not made by dog, cat, bird or rat. There are also Maori traditions of an animal like a beaver on the West Coast, so that, perhaps, Cook was right after all.

Not long ago, a coffin was found containing a skeleton, with some remnants of clothes about it, and a pig-tail on the skull. So far as could be judged, the clothes and pig-tail were similar to those worn by officers in the days of Cook. What gives additional strength to this theory is that near the coffin were found an old flint musket and an axe.

In Facile Harbour, a snug little shelter on Revolution Island, near Cormorant Cove, can be seen an old sunken ship. She is about 180 feet long, copper-bottomed, rests on her keel, and a portion of her deck could be seen at low water projecting above the surface. There is much speculation as to what she was.

Pat, of course, was able to supply us with a tradition concerning the ill-fated craft, for he has spent many years sealing and knocking about these sounds, and few men living know more about them, or have heard more of their traditions. Pat can pitch a twister, for fun, with anybody, but I have always found his statements as to places and events reliable; and I believe that his version of the derelict ship is as likely to be true as any other.

The ship, according to this Irish authority, was an East Indiaman, called the "Endymion," which put into Facile Harbour in a sinking condition. The exact date of the "Endymion's" arrival is uncertain; but an old Maori named Soloman, who lives at Riverton, in Southland, New Zealand, says that when he was a boy he was in Facile Harbour with his father when the "Endymion" arrived.

Now, the Maories are said to live to a great age, and it is hard to tell how long it is since Solomon was a boy. I once saw an old Maori on the West Coast of the North Island, who looked like a piece of tattooed parchment drawn over a skeleton. He was the oldest-looking and most shrivelled-up specimen of humanity it ever fell to my lot to see. I was shown the decayed trunk of a very large pine tree, which had died from old age, and was told that that self-same Maori was an old man when that tree was beginning to grow. The tree had been about four feet in diameter and I put that Maori down at 300 or 400, because it is only very young men or people who have not travelled much who are so foolish as to contradict what they are told. Solomon may be like this old man, but I am inclined to think that what he really meant to say was that, when his father was a young man, the ill-fated East Indiaman came into Facile Harbour. What induces me to think so is the fact that I have known the Maories to talk about what their ancestors did and saw as if it actually had reference to themselves. Anyhow, leaving out the question of date, the tradition goes on to say, that the " Endymion " had a large crew of Indians on board (Lascars), and a few white men; that she was in a very leaky condition, and that the crew hove her down to enable them, if possible, to get at the leak. However, in carrying out this operation, the vessel unfortunately capsized and sank. The crew got away in boats and rafts. The white men took the long boat and left the sound, and were not again heard of. Their fate to this day remains a mystery, though it can easily be imagined. The Indians made their way towards the south, taking much the same course as we had taken from Cormorant Cove, and landed on Endymion Island, as the Maories call it, and which, I think, must be the island marked " Indian Island" on the chart made by Her Majesty's ship "Acheron" in 1851.

Indian Island is about one-and-a-half miles south of Resolution Island, and three-quarters of a mile west of Long Island, and would be right in the track of the Indians if they were making their way south down Resolution Island and through the passage between it and Anchor Island. The sound here teems with islands, some of them abounding with the tutu plant to which I have already referred. One of those islets near Indian Island is called Poison Island from that reason, and the Indians are said to have landed on it and, eating largely of the tutu berries, many of them died.

These poor castaways moved from island to island, finally

stopping on Anchor Island. From this island they would stand the best chance of seeing any passing ship, and would as well be able to get good shelter. It is supposed they had no boats, and had to depend on rafts for navigating purposes. That certainly would account for their making no effort to leave the sheltered waters of the sound. The last of them is said to have died of poison and starvation on Anchor Island, and there is a cave on the island yet full of their bones. Pat once went sealing with two white men and a Maori, found this cave, and saw the bleaching remains of the unfortunate seamen. The skeletons were a good deal covered with earth, and seemed to be lying as if the men had been huddled together when death came to rescue them from their miserable fate. Pat wanted to clear away the dirt and have a look at them, but the Maori, like all Maories, had a dread of touching or allowing to be touched anything pertaining to the dead, said they were Tapu—which, being interpreted, means sacred—and was in such a state of excitement in case they touched any of the bones, and thereby aroused the anger of the spirits, that they cleared out of the cave without carrying out their intentions. Our companion said he was quite prepared to take anyone to the cave. I got him to mark out its position on the chart, and intend to visit it before long.

There are various other traditions about the skeletons. All agree that they are those of the Indians, but some differ as to the manner by which their death was compassed, alleging that the Maories, who were numerous in those days, killed and ate them after having taken them to the cave for the express purpose of indulging their cannibalistic instincts.

Some say the wreck is not that of the "Endymion" but the "Endeavour," lost in 1793, about which Dr. Hocken of Dunedin, recently read a very interesting paper at Dunedin at a meeting of the Otago Branch of the New Zealand Institute. Again, I have been told on good authority that the celebrated navigator, Bass, sailed from Sydney for South America in 1803. Before sailing he wrote to a friend saying that he should call at Dusky Sound, New Zealand, to take copper and other things from a sunken ship he knew of there, which he would be able to sell to the Spaniards in South America. Bass was never heard of again. From this we may conclude that the wreck in Facile Harbour was there before 1803. I afterwards visited this old wreck, and we pulled some of her up. I have specimens of her timber and copper in my possession.

In talking about Maori superstitions, Pat told me that on one occasion when fossicking about in Pickersgill Cove, Dusky Sound, he and his mates found what looked to be a grave. The mound was neatly made and fenced in with supple-jacks interlaced, their ends being fixed in the ground. At the head of the mound was a wooden cross, and on this cross was carved "Sacred to the Memory of Poor Old Potatoes." Pat got a spade and started digging, to see, as he said, what Poor Old Potatoes was like. He found nothing but the stump of a tree. He heard afterwards that a prospector had hid some stores there, and made a grave to keep the Maories off. The Maories have a great fear of graves, and will not touch or go near them in case the spirits of the departed should get angry and do them harm.

Dusky Sound is seldom visited by whalers now; indeed, the industry seems nearly dead in this part of the world. There are still a few seals to be found about the islands and rocks, chiefly near the mouth of the sound. Its waters teem with fish, more sometimes than at others. Our efforts this day were rewarded with the capture of a few blue cod and soldier fish. These latter are like carp, with large coarse scales, of a golden red colour, but they are of no use for eating purposes.

After the candles were lighted in the little cabin, the skipper, C., E., and self killed the evening over a friendly game at euchre, the soothing breath of the poisonous demon nicotine, and conversation of a more or less animated character, finally finishing up with a glass of beer, and turning in about 10 p.m.

CHAPTER VIII.

Departure from Duck Cove.—A Boating Expedition.—Imposing
Mountain Scenery. —Visit to Docherty's Hut.—A Hermit Life.
—More Prospecting and Unrequited Labour.—A Hard Pull
in a Half Gale.—The Search for the "Rosa."—Wet Jacket
Arm and its Giant Mountains and Cascades.—A Gorgeous
Sunset.—Once again on Board the Cutter.

NEXT day, the 24th November, we lay at anchor, it blowing a strong gale of wind from the south.

I spent most of the time rowing from point to point, landing
and prospecting. We found large masses of white felspar
rock, and it is not unlikely that the mare's tail up the mountain side which I have described is composed of it. Further,
a considerable quantity of iron pyrites and a few traces of
copper were discovered. Wherever we landed the sand-flies
immediately gathered around and commenced their blood-
thirsty attacks. On board the "Rosa" a few fish were caught.
The wind died away at evening, and the sky cleared, with the
result that we had a beautiful sunset. As the breeze died
away, sand-flies came on board and fed on us till darkness
set in.

Next day broke very fine, not a cloud in the sky, with a
light cool breeze stealing down from the mountains.

At 5 a.m. we weighed anchor, and were soon gliding once
more over the scarcely ruffled blue waters of Duck Cove. The
bright invigorating air was full of the musical melody of singing birds; magnificent mountains towered around us, with
every outline standing out remarkably clear and distinct; and

overhead the atmosphere was as deep a blue as sky could well be. It was altogether a very beautiful scene, one not easily to be forgotten.

We had been so long delayed that we decided to push on to Big Bay, just calling at Wet-Jacket Arm, Dusky Sound, and having a look at Milford Sound on account of its far-famed beauty. The morning breeze soon began to fail, and we did no more than creep out of the cove into the main sound before it fell dead calm.

It was now nine o'clock, and we had only made about three miles. We got out the boats and tried the experiment of towing the cutter, but soon gave it up, the result achieved not being commensurate with the trouble taken. Then we tried fishing, and caught some excellent blue cod. We lay beclamed in the most enchanting scenery imaginable, basking in a hot sun. Without a motion we rested on the still, deep, blue waters of the sound, studded with its countless green islands; shut in on all sides by huge mountains, with their uniform 3000-feet mantle of dark bush dipping into the water, and their numerous rocky snow-covered peaks towering every-where.

There being no signs of a breeze, C., E., O. and self, with two of the Danes, started in the whale-boat to pull about eight miles up the main arm of the sound to where a man named Docherty has a hut, and where he has lived chiefly by himself for several years, passing his time in cutting tracks and exploring the mountains for minerals.

There are two or three men who lead this solitary kind of life on the West Coast. Government sends a steamer round the New Zealand coast once every three months to take stores to the lighthouses, and also to call at any place where men are staying. Stores are always obtainable from the steamer on payment. The stores consist chiefly of flour, salt, tea, and tinned or cured meat. But these wanderers from the centres of civilisation live, as a rule, on little else except fish and native birds, of which they can catch any quantity if they have good dogs. Docherty, from time to time, turns up at Dunedin with specimens of minerals he has found, and has often got money to help him to open up the lodes, but hitherto nothing has come of any of his finds. He has struck upon one vein of copper ore, which, perhaps, it may pay to work some day. Before I left Dunedin he had been there and reported having found a large deposit of nickel ore, and had got a little help towards testing its value. I have been asked by some people interested to look at the deposit and form an opinion as to its worth. For this purpose I had the plan of the hut and the position of the mine in my possession. I was told that a track had been cut to the mine and five tons of stuff brought down.

We left the cutter at half-past nine, it being arranged that if a breeze sprung up we would turn back, the cutter meantime waiting for us off the south point of Resolution Island. The boat was an easy one to pull, and with smooth water and four oars going we made good progress. There were six of us in her, and all were used to rowing but one. He sat and looked about him, while the other took the steer oar, and so all were occupied. It was easy work with the steer oar, and for this reason we took turn and turn about at it. We passed island after island, scaring numerous flocks of ducks and divers. As we advanced the high mountains at the head of the sound became more conspicuous, but otherwise the scenery was unchanged, the wall-like, bush-clad mountains coming steep down to the water on each side of the sound. Past Promontory Creek and Bay we, gaily talking, pulled our way. The only thing which troubled us was the heat, which became excessive. We were in 45° 48′ south latitude, about the same distance from the equator as the south of France, and within four weeks of the longest day. Thus the sun was pretty high up at noon, and its rays most powerful. In many places the mountains descended so steeply into the water that for long distances we could not have landed our boat even had we wanted to, although it would have been easy enough to have tied her to the boughs of the overhanging trees which clung to the precipitous sides.

The sound varied from two to four miles across. To the right were two large islands, called respectively Long and Cooper Islands, both mountainous and timber-clad to the very summit; behind and above these towered the mountains on the mainland. Equally high were the mountains on our left, and we were, each moment, getting closer to and more hemmed in than ever by the giant masses at the head of the sound.

The weather kept still and hot, and at noon we found ourselves at Docherty's. He has three well-built huts, and a little above a good boat-landing, situated in a beautiful white sand and pebble-beached bay through which a clear and limpid

F

mountain stream empties itself into the sound. As we approached the landing, the white sand and stones forming the bed of the sound could be seen at a great depth through the crystal, translucent water. Immediately behind the huts the mountains are very precipitous. The view looking out to the sound from the shore was as majestic a combination of mountains, forest, coast line, islands and blue water as one could possibly imagine.

At one point, about 1,200 feet above, and a little to the west of the huts, the bush seemed to have been cleared off the face of the rock for some distance, and parallel quartz veins, assumed to be about two feet thick, could be seen coming down the cliff in a perpendicular position. The rock and stone about the beach were chiefly composed of hard, laminated schist, with fragments of granite and quartz.

We found the huts empty, except for swarms of sand-flies. These pests, the moment we landed, crowded round, and commenced an old colonial habit of "drinks all round" at our expense. We discovered a well-made track, leading up a gully through the bush behind the huts, and followed it for over two miles. Here we came upon a face of solid granite, with thin quartz veins and small pockets of garnets cropping out. The formation was very much the same as that we had seen at Resolution Island. We discovered no trace of minerals, and, a breeze setting in, we returned to the boat after a couple of hours' fossicking.

Upon re-embarking, we soon became aware of the fact that we had a fresh and still freshening breeze against us, and pulling was rather stiff work. The men said the breeze would soon fall, and proposed that we should land somewhere and have lunch. I expected the breeze would last to sunset, but after we had pulled about two miles from Docherty's, a most delightful little bay induced me to consent to land for the purpose of partaking of the mid-day meal.

I could not help thinking, as we pulled away from Docherty's hermit home, that men like him, who could live year after year alone in such an isolated spot, beautiful though it be, worried by sand-flies by day all the year round, and for several months by mosquitoes at night, cutting tracks through the dark, silent, New Zealand bush, searching for wealth, which, if they find it, will most likely benefit others more than themselves, deserve admiration and encouragement, even though they may work to no purpose. Our Anglo-Saxon race has produced many such men, who devote their lives to sowing in the wilderness the seeds of future wealth and greatness, the fruit of which is reaped by the nations which follow in their footsteps.

We had lunch just at the edge of the bush, close to the sparkling water. Spreading boughs intervened between us and the hot sun; a pleasant breeze tempered the heat and kept the sand-flies away; while numberless birds, revelling in the warmth and beauty of a summer day, gave us music while we ate.

We next prospected up the bed of a small creek which runs into the harbour. Its bottom rock is hard, laminated schist, with here and there veins of quartz, some of the latter more than a foot thick and containing masses of mica. We washed out several pockets, but got no trace of gold, although there were what diggers call indications. The beach was strewn with fragments of iron-stained quartz.

On re-embarking the wind had freshened up to a strong breeze, and the sound was churned into a mass of white water. Pulling under such circumstances was hard work, and steering not easy. I soon saw symptoms of distress in the faces of the crew, the big Dane especially, and upon my taking his oar, he muttered a heart-felt "thank God!" I really believe he could not have pulled much longer.

In spite of all difficulties we stuck resolutely to our oars, and eventually crept up to where the cutter ought to have been, but was not. I supposed that the skipper had run for shelter to Wet-Jacket Arm, ten miles away, and blessed him for so doing, especially as there was no real need for the shifting of the anchorage. However, we had nothing to do but follow. We had now come about eight miles from Docherty's, in a nearly west course; and, to reach the mouth of Wet-Jacket Arm, would have to pull about four miles due north, up Acheron Passage, between the east side of Resolution Island and the mainland; while from the mouth to the head of the Arm would be about six miles more. I was pretty certain the skipper had gone to the head of the Arm, because he had told me there was no good anchorage nearer than that. We had some hopes that when we got into Acheron Passage the wind might be drawing up it, and so be favourable; but as we entered we found half a gale or more blowing right in our teeth, and causing a nasty, choppy sea. The boat was a good one, and, with a trained and stalwart crew, there would have been no difficulty in accomplishing the task; but our men were not much used to rough water, and did not seem to relish the four mile pull right into the black and angry sea ahead of us. The Danes were anxious to land and bush it for the night. This I would not hear of though. I took the stroke oar, and directing the man at the helm to keep us over to the west side of the passage, where we would be more sheltered, we lay to with the oars. Our jackets and everything else we had on were soon drenched through and through, but at last we got opposite to the mouth of Wet-Jacket Arm. We had now to cross the passage, about a mile wide, through a heavy beam sea in half a gale of wind, before we could get into Wet-Jacket Arm, and again it was proposed to land for the night. I was sure that once we were in Wet-Jacket Arm, we should find smooth water and a fair wind. So I took the helm, told them to pull on, and away again we started. All went well. We dodged the heavy seas, plunged across, tugged round a point, and entered the Arm, passing in a few yards from a stormy sea and adverse wind into smooth water, with the additional advantage of a light, fair breeze gently setting up the Arm. We could see nothing of the cutter, but far away up the Arm appeared a white speck in the sunshine, looking no bigger than a pocket-handkerchief, and which, as we watched it, glided across the sound and disappeared, soon to appear again, smaller still, and then vanish for good. No hull or mast could be seen, and so diminutive was the white speck, that I was generally laughed at when I said it was the cutter running up the Arm with a fresh breeze behind her. They would not have it, and said it might be the sail of some small boat, or perhaps was only a sea-gull.

I may remark here, that a stranger to these sounds finds himself utterly at a loss to form any adequate idea of the heights or distances; so clear is the atmosphere and vast the surroundings that even trained eyes are completely deceived. I have known waterfalls computed by experienced men at 70 feet, which on actual measurement proved over 500. I have started to pull to a point which looked but scarcely a mile away, and after half-an-hour steady rowing in smooth water seemed to be not much nearer. We found afterwards that the speck was the cutter, five miles off, she anchoring at the head of the Arm just when we saw the speck finally disappear.

Some of the crew were sure the cutter had not gone up the Arm, but had most likely gone back to Duck Cove, and insisted that our best plan was to land and pass the night in the bush, and look for the cutter in the morning. By this time the sun was getting low, and night would be on in a couple of hours or so. " Cutter or phantom, boat or gull, or whatever that speck was," said I, " I'm going to look for it, if I go to the head of the Arm to night. If it's not the cutter but some other boat we will find them and get a bite of something, which will be better than passing the night in the bush without food to eat or a blanket to cover us." With this, I took the stroke oar, and bade my men row on.

We were now entering one of the grandest pieces of scenery the West Coast of New Zealand has to show. Wet-Jacket Arm, though six miles long, is nowhere a mile wide, and the mountains rise on each side like sheer walls to a height of from 4,000 to 6,000 feet, 3,000 feet of which is clothed with dense forest, save where, in many places, it is so steep that nothing but lichen, moss, and small ferns can cling to the perpendicular sides. Numerous cascades, rising from close to the highest points, can be seen from near their sources, like silver threads interwoven with grey rock and green bush, tumbling down every face. Although appearing to the eye like the finest threads, yet were you close to many of them you would find them rushing torrents difficult to cross. The setting sun now tinted the mountain peaks with glorious hues, and, as the breeze died away, their majestic outlines were reproduced on the surface of the deep still water over which we propelled our boat. We seemed, indeed, to be cutting our way through a liquid mirror. About half way up, and on the north side of the Arm, is a little island, circular in shape, about 10 acres in extent, and 300 feet high, covered with timber. So vast is the surrounding scale of nature's grandeur, that one would hardly take the island to be more than 40 feet in height, and such our crew considered it to be. As we neared it, a piece of timber not unlike the top of a ship's mast was discerned, apparently projecting above the bush on the far side of the island, and it was hailed by our men as the mast of the cutter. They were confident that if we pulled round the island we should find the cutter at anchor under the other side. I remarked that the object was but the top of a dead tree, and that it was at least 200 feet above us. They got more positive it was the ship's mast as we got nearer, and one of them declared, with all seriousness, that he could see it move.   I was quite certain in my own mind that the cutter was at anchor three miles away, at the head of the Arm, but as I had no objection to the extra half-mile pull which going inside the island involved, and was, indeed, not unwilling to thus prolong our journey in such beautiful weather as it now was and among such imposing scenery, I consented, and round we went.   We found its nearest point not more than 200 yards from the mainland.   As we rounded each point the men kept saying, "We shall see the cutter round the next point;" but point after point was passed, till we had pulled round the island, and still no cutter! At nearly the highest point of the island, however, a bare, branchless, pole-like trunk of a dead tree could be plainly seen projecting above the surrounding bush.   My surmise had thus been correct.   The hopeful ones now became silent, and pulled on for the head of the Arm without saying much.   As we proceeded, the Arm gradually got narrower, and the mountains higher and even more precipitous.   Their grandeur was only intensified by the golden light of a glorious sunset.

Such a scene might be painted, but the man never lived who could find words adequate to its description.   Could Longfellow have beheld such a scene, he would have died gazing at it, murmuring "Excelsior," and trying in vain to imagine a youth with a banner, fit to be in keeping with its beauty, as he passed from one gilded peak to another.   Tennyson would break his heart, being unable to find words sufficient to describe its manifold glories.   Too grand a frame even for his picture of the "Passing of Arthur;" too beautiful to receive without detraction the saintly form of his fair dead maiden drifting by on her flower-decked barge.   And had any of the world's greatest landscape painters, ancient or modern, been present, they would have felt that their noblest works were but vanity, and have prayed for a recurrence of the miracle of Joshua—that the sun might be stayed in his course, at least till they had transferred to canvas the magnificent outline of earth's masses which surrounded them, the glorious flood of light which illumined this enchanting scene, and the still surface of water which so faithfully mirrored this wonderful grouping of the Creator's works.

But we were neither artists or poets, only very ordinary mortals, and not at all in the frame of mind that would incline us to go into raptures about the gigantic distortions of the earth's crust by which we were surrounded. Even had we been so minded, our raptures would have been effectually crushed in the bud by the fact that we were tired, hungry and thirsty; that darkness was setting in; and that we were uncertain how long we might have to keep tugging away at our oars before we arrived at food or shelter, or if we should even find them at all that night. So we scarcely spoke, looked at little save each other's backs, or the bottom of the boat, as we doggedly worked at our oars, and only occasionally turned to see if there was any appearance of the head of the Arm being near, or the cutter in view.

Just as the last of the sun's rays were fading from the highest peaks, and the shades of night were beginning to brood over the waters and along the base of the bush-clad mountains, we rounded a point, to find ourselves immediately after in a little bay forming the head of the Arm. And there, too, most gladsome of sights, not half-a-mile away, lay the cutter " Rosa" peacefully at anchor. We hailed her with loud cheers, and pulling with renewed vigour, were soon once again on board our floating home, where a much-needed meal was hastily prepared.

CHAPTER IX.

THE FEATHERED SONGSTER'S CONCERT.—A CHAT ABOUT NEW ZEALAND
BIRDS.—AN EXPLORATION PARTY.—A MOUNTAIN RAIN-STORM.—
A NOVEL FRESH-WATER BATH.—FISHING UNDER DIFFICULTIES.—
A PANORAMA OF MOUNTAIN CATARACTS.—PRODIGIOUS RAINFALL.
—THE VOYAGE OF THE "ROSA" IS RESUMED.—SABBATH REFLEC-
TIONS.—BEATING DOWN CHANNEL.

HERE, at the head of the Arm, the mountains which had
been gradually getting higher and grander, culminated
in a magnificent amphitheatre of Titanic peaks, having an
attitude of over 5,000 feet, and forming huge walls which
seemed to completely envelope us. On their almost perpendicular sides bush and rock struggle for the mastery; down
countless green and rock-flecked precipices drop fairy cascades like crystal feathers waving over walls of emerald
and marble; and, far away and above, snow-robed peaks soar
in high air.

A truly splendid spectacle, and not a breath of wind or
ripple on the water, save where wild fowl disport themselves.
A solemn stillness reigns in the atmosphere, broken only by
the ceaseless murmur of countless waterfalls—nature's organ
playing at eventide in one of her grandest cathedrals. Hungry
as I was, I stayed on deck some time before going down to
tea, knowing that, ere I came up again, the mountains
would be almost hidden in the deepening shadows of the
night, and that all the glory of the sunlight would have passed
away.

I was not at all pleased with the skipper running away from us as he had. He made a lame excuse about the strength of the wind, and the want of good anchorage anywhere else. My own opinion was he wanted to get an evening's fishing and shooting at the head of the Arm. I found out to my cost afterwards that one needed to keep a very sharp eye on the skipper. Tea quite refreshed us after our pull of 28 miles, and as soon as we had disposed of the welcome meal we assembled on deck to make the most of a scene so unique—one such as we might never have the opportunity of seeing again.

As the darkness came on, the native birds gave us a concert. The soft, prolonged whistle of the kiwi, the weird wailing call of the weka, the clear whistle and harsh screech of the kaka, the still harsher screech of kakapo, the scream of the penguin, and the plaintiff hoot of the morepork owl were all heard in discordant unison, more or less, through the early hours of the night. We fired a gun, and the report came back in a chorus of thunder-peals.

Our conversation turned chiefly upon the New Zealand birds and their habits. M. spoke of a bird he once heard at Murdering Beach, near Longbush, in Southland. It came at night, and set up a most unearthly scream, weird, wild, horrifying; but he did not succeed in getting a view of his unwelcome and uncongenial visitor. The Maories about there say it is white in colour but never seen, and that it is a spirit; when they hear it, they hide themselves. In the beginning of 1882 two friends and myself were camped on the shore of Lake Hauroto, an unfrequented and almost unknown sheet of water, surrounded by high mountains, in the south-west of the South Island. One night we were roused by a most unearthly noise, which, to me, resembled the screams of a human being in dire agony. We went outside our tent, and found the scream proceeded from high up in a tall tree near at hand. I took my gun, and lay for some time under the tree, trying, if I could, to catch an outline of the screamer. I could detect an occasional movement of the branches at one particular spot, and at last I fired in that direction. A large bird then flew away, its wings making a noise resembling that of a swift in its flight, and we heard it no more, nor have I ever heard anything like it since. I have made inquiries among some of the oldest residents on the West Coast about this bird, and some have never even heard of it. Others have heard it, or heard of it. Some Maories reported that it has a long tail and wings, and flies so fast that you can hardly get a glimpse of it in its flight. Further, they said its plumage is most gorgeous, As it is a night bird, however, I doubt the last statement. I, myself, imagine it to be some kind of night hawk. We turned into our bunks rather late.

Next morning was bright and warm, with electrical clouds very high up passing from the north-west. The sky presented the same appearance as it does in Canterbury or Otago when a hot north-west wind is blowing. At early morn the native birds were making a pleasing chorus, conspicuous among them being the bell-bird, tuis, and robin, the latter singing in a style sufficient to make even nightingales jealous. Although aware that the robin was no mean songster, I had no idea how well he could sing till I heard him on the West Coast, and the first day I listened to the sweet notes in Dusky Sound I doubted if it were a robin. M. was positive it was, and to settle the matter he and I got into the dingy and rowed under the spreading boughs of a tree, amongst which a songster was making melody. We soon got sight of him, and it proved to be a robin sure enough.

After breakfast all hands went ashore. The extraordinary height and steepness of the mountains seemed in no wise diminished when seen in the bright light of morning, as contrasted with our first view of them at sunset on the previous evening, and this was especially apparent as we rowed close under them on our way to the shore. Looking up you would see right overhead a silver thread, apparently thrown over the rock, and could hardly conceive that it was a considerable body of water tumbling over the rocks 4,000 feet above. Many of the mountain sides are sheer perpendicular walls of rock, painted green with moss and small ferns for 3,000 feet, and quite bare above that elevation. In many places you can touch the mountain sides with the bow of the boat, and if you dropped a line over the stern you would hardly find the bottom at 10 fathoms.

Upon landing, our party and the Captain's joined together for a good fossick, our object being to find a lagoon said to exist a mile or two back in the bush. The Captain, however, did not seem to care for the work, and growled like a bear, but as his men were determined to go on he could not very well turn back. However, after we had proceeded about half-a-mile he gave up and went back to the cutter, the rest keeping on. We cut our way about a mile-and-a-half through the bush, keeping above and not far from the bed of a creek which flows into the head of the Arm. The bush was composed chiefly of moderately sized birch, with light undergrowth ; the chief impediment to progress being large quantities of fallen and rotting timber. When we ultimately arrived at the lagoon we found it to be nothing but a pond situated in a swamp, with a few acres of open grass country about it, and a quantity of white everlasting flowers growing amongst the grass. The sight of this open country so raised the spirits of Tom the sailor that he immediately turned head over heels several times.

Here we lighted a fire and boiled a billy which Pat had brought with him, made tea, and had our midday meal, after which we proceeded with our exploration. We pushed on up the creek, and found that it terminated in a series of cascades which tumbled in a few falls close upon 3,000 feet. After this we retraced our steps, keeping mostly to the bed of the creek, scrambling over large boulders, splashing through the water, and occasionally having to leave the bed of the river and force our way through the bush.

The day was very hot, and I had a dip in a clear deep pool. I found the water very cold and pleasant, but, unfortunately, the sand-flies also discovered me to be very nice, and as the result I suffered a good deal before I had dressed. We got back to the cutter about half-past five. During this ramble we sunk several holes, and washed out many dishes, but found nothing but black iron-sand, fragments of pink garnet, and a few specimens of white marble. Of birds, we saw blue and paradise ducks, crows, canaries, robins, wekas, and one kea (flesh-eating mountain parrot). It turned a close, dull, calm night, with a few drops of rain.

Next morning at 4.30 a.m. I went on deck, and heard the most extraordinary chorus of singing birds I ever listened to in my life. The air was full of sound as if millions of anvils were being struck with tiny hammers. The effect was indescribable, but most enjoyable. It was the bell-birds chanting their morning song ; their notes bear no little resemblance to the tinkling of silver bells. Judging from the volume of sound, one would almost think that every tree or bush in the dense forest clothing the mountain sides had one of these feathered warblers for an occupant.

I went overboard for my usual swim, and then about 6 a.m. a tremendous downpour of rain commenced. The clouds, which since daylight had been hanging thick and black, high up, and apparently touching the highest of the mountain peaks, seemed suddenly to burst. The mountains at first disappeared, and then loomed through a thick haze, while the rain came down in sheets.

Some of us took advantage of the opportunity to have a fresh-water bath by simply standing undressed on deck. The deck was soon an inch or two deep in water, caused by the fact that the rain was not able to get away as quickly as it fell. Unfortunately the deck seams were not very tight, and it was not long before the cabin ceiling began to drip all over. This necessitated buckets, pannikins, and dishes being placed to catch the downpour in various places.

After breakfast E. and I put on oilskins and gum boots—the latter reaching up to the hips—and went fishing in the dingy. It was dead calm, and the surface of the water was covered with large bubbles made by the splash of the heavy rain. We pulled round a rocky point out of sight of the cutter, and put out our lines; although only a few feet from the shore we could not bottom with 20 fathoms. We shifted into a little bay, and near the centre of it, at about 10 yards from the shore, got on the bottom, and immediately caught fish.

Such was the volume of water now pouring into the sound from innumerable torrents foaming down the mountain sides that we found a strong surface fresh-water current setting down the sound at quite two miles an hour. This kept carrying us into deep water, as we had no anchor or rope with which to make our boat fast to the trees; and, as we could get no fish where we did not bottom, we had constantly to suspend operations and pull back to shallow water. Thus we spent several hours not unpleasantly, E. being a first-rate companion. We landed once or twice, but found the sand-flies so savage that we were glad to take to our boat again. These pests were apparently not in anyway put about by a downpour which one would have imagined quite capable of washing them all away. They seemed, in fact, to move slowly about among the thick rain drops without being touched by them. So heavy was the downpour that we had constantly to bale the water out of the dingy, but our oilskins and long boots kept us quite dry.

The mountain sides, where clear of bush, seemed in many places to be positively sheeted with flowing water, and the cascades thundering into the basin on all sides constituted a sight ever to be remembered. We caught some fine blue cod, white fish, and red soldiers, and returned to the cutter about midday with fish enough for all hands. The remainder of the day was spent in smoking, yarning and playing cards. Just at sunset I counted 40 large cascades within a mile of the cutter, falling over 3,000 feet of sheer precipice. The noise, I need scarcely state, was deafening. A white mist settled on the mountain as night came on, and soon after the rain stopped.

I have no doubt that at least a foot of rain fell during the day. I measured the next rainfall of a similar sort that we had later on in Milford Sound. I then ascertained the record to stand at over 20 inches between sunrise and sunset.

The cabin after this deluge of rain was decidedly damp, and we had, on turning in, to put oilskins over our blankets to keep the drips off. E. and O. had decidedly the worst sleeping places. They lay with their heads close to the rudder, well under, and only a few inches from the cutter's deck, their upper parts resting on the sloping lining of the ship's stern, and their lower extremities upon planks thrown across a couple of boxes which stood on the cabin floor.

Next morning, Sunday, the 28th November, broke calm and beautiful, with a cloudless sky and a few patches of white mist resting here and there about the mountains. The atmosphere was wonderfully clear after the rain, and showed up the marvellous panorama to perfection.

We weighed anchor at 6 a.m., C. and I first going overboard for a good swim ; we found the water quite fresh. There was a dead calm, and we again had to row the cutter. In the absence of proper sweeps, our progress was perforce very slow.

After breakfast and a turn at the oars I went below, having the cabin to myself, and, as is my custom on Sunday, commenced reading the Bible. Somehow, as I read, I seemed to drift away to Berwick-on-Tweed in company with an old friend, listening to Dr. Cairns. Voices called to me over the waves of time—voices, when I thought I was alone, telling me I, who could not see, was seen by some I knew and loved, and had loved and lost, and saying that I, who walked with those who walked with God, was still allowed at intervals to hear the voice which guided them to brighter worlds. A score of years have rolled away, and memory, touched by the words of Holy Writ, is walking in the paths my father trod; waits in his church and listens to God's word; passes through the streets which he as a schoolboy knew, and meets and converses with his kith and kin. Those long dead seem speaking in my ear; hands which the graveyard holds seem clasping mine. Then some one comes down the steps into the cabin, and the spell is broken.

Once again I come back to life in the small, damp cabin of the " Rosa," riding a calm inland sea in New Zealand, compassed by towering mountains o'er which countless foaming cataracts swollen by yesterday's rain are thundering down a rocky descent of 4,000 sheer feet into the tranquil waters of Wet-Jacket Arm.

Presently a slight breeze sprang up, and we slowly beat down the inlet. Most of us busied ourselves drying wet clothes, &c., and making things comfortable after the discomforts to which we had been exposed by the wiles of Pluvius.

At 5 p.m. we anchored under a small island in Acheron Passage, just at the mouth and to the north side of Wet-Jacket Arm. Acheron Passage is situated between Resolution Island and the mainland. It is about eight miles in length, and joins Breaksea to Dusky Sound. It was up this passage we had our hardest pull on the occasion of our visit to Docherty's in the whale-boat. We let go the anchor over the cutter's bow, and fastened the stern of the stout little craft to trees on the mainland with ropes. As we were on the point of going ashore, the Captain called two of his dogs to go with him, thinking they might catch some birds. One refused to come, and upon the Captain taking hold of her to lift her into the boat the animal bit his hand. He dropped the offending canine immediately, looked at his hand, became profane, danced like a madman, and finished up by rushing at the slut like a wild beast and flinging her far away into the water, where she would have drowned had not Tom the sailor got into one of the boats, gone to the rescue, and hauled her out. If she had been mine, I must say I think I should have put a shot in her.

We spent the evening fishing and prospecting. The rocks were chiefly granite, shewing thin veins of yellow mica. This mica is common in several of the sounds, sometimes occurring in large quantities. When seen at the bottom of streams and pools of water it has very much the appearance of gold; it is sometimes called "New Chum's Gold." We found three varieties of marble—two pure white, and the other grey-veined. In one of the white pieces were small particles of very white soft metal. Several blue cod were caught, and M. hooked a large groper which gave him a good deal of play. One of the men got hold of it with a gaff and partly lifted it out of the water, but let it off, and it finally broke away. I should say it weighed quite 40 lbs.

The groper or hapuka is very common on these coasts; it is generally caught about 10 or 20 lbs. in weight, sometimes much heavier. I have been told that they not unfrequently attain a weight of 200 lbs. The New Zealand Fishing Act does not allow them to be killed under 5 lbs. They are something like a cod in appearance; their flesh is white and very solid. Groper cutlet is not bad by any means when one is hungry or has not tasted fish for some time. They are a coarse fish, and about the cheapest sold in the Dunedin market. I cannot say I care much for them myself. The flesh is often affected with trichina, and unless it is well cooked these worms remain alive in it. A friend of mine, a medical man in Dunedin, one day when out at dinner, took a piece of groper unobserved from his plate and placed it in his pocket. On making an examination at home he found it to contain several live trichina.

CHAPTER X.

NEXT morning we weighed anchor and untied our ropes at
six. Then with a pleasant breeze we stood to the north
up Acheron Passage (named after Her Majesty's ship
" Acheron," which in 1850-51 surveyed these sounds), and
after sailing about four miles we entered Breaksea Sound.

The mountains on both sides of Acheron Passage are steep
and lofty, covered with the usual forest, and some fine cascades are to be seen, especially on the mainland. The passage
runs about a mile wide, and for a long distance. Although a
small boat could be tied up to the trees, yet it was impossible
to land, so steeply and abruptly do the mountains rise out of
the water. A fine specimen of a sea tree was dredged up in
this passage after our visit.

The sea tree is a kind of seaweed which grows attached to
rocks below low-water line. It has branches, is hard and
black as ebony, and in shape and appearance resembles a
stag's horn.

We had now left Dusky Sound. I have several times
visited this sound since, as well as nearly all the other sounds,

and have come to the conclusion that this sound will ultimately become far and away the favourite haunt with tourists. From whatever quarter the wind may blow, there is always some spot in Dusky Sound where, probably surrounded by beautiful islands, the pleasure-seeker will find shelter from rude old Boreas, and be able to fish in smooth water or otherwise amuse himself. On the other hand, in most of the other sounds, including Milford, the wind often sweeps over their whole surface with such violence, for days together, as to put boating on them for pleasure purposes quite out of the question. The scenery is also more varied in this sound than in any other, being pretty and pleasing to the eye, as well as terribly grand. The mountainous head of Wet-Jacket Arm is as wild a piecc of scenery as anything to be found in the sounds; while nothing can be more charming and beautiful than to sail among the islands to the south and about Resolution Island. In Cormorant Cove and Facile Harbour the scenery strikingly resembles that of the English lakes, if you could only imagine the Cumberland and Westmoreland hills covered with dense, dark green forest. Another perfect gem in the way of scenic effect is Pickersgill or Cook's Harbour, about five miles from South Point as you enter the sound from the south. A lofty wooded island, called Crayfish, lies across the mouth of a little bay forming the harbour. The passage between the west of Crayfish and the mainland is not more than 50 yards wide, with high wooded cliffs on each side; on the left several hundred, and on the right over 2,000 feet above the sea level. On entering the harbour through this passage, a beautiful view opens itself to the admiring gaze of the traveller. The harbour is a sheet of deep water about half-a-mile wide, opening to the east. Looking up this opening, one sees mile after mile of blue water dotted with islands, hemmed in with huge green mountains, behind which rise pile after pile of peaks robed in eternal snow.

In October, 1888, when in Facile Harbour with the Government steamer, I saw the Captain succeed in raising several pieces of the old wreck of which in a previous chapter I have already said much. Eleven pieces—being portions of the upper deck beams—were safely got on board the steamer. The timber was teak, and some of the pieces measured 22 feet in length, with a breadth and thickness of 14 inches by 12.

Breaksea Sound runs in an easterly direction 10 miles, and

G

then branches into two forks, each fork being about six miles in length and its general breadth a little over a mile.

Its waters are very deep, as much as 288 fathoms in places. Almost at the head of the south fork a depth of 127 fathoms is found, and 97 at the head of the north one. The head water of the north fork is but three miles distant from the head water of Hall's Arm in Smith's Sound. The head of Hall's Arm is about 23 miles from the entrance to Doubtful Sound, of which it is a continuation, while again the mouth of Doubtful Sound is some 20 miles further up the coast than the mouth of Breaksea. We did not go into Breaksea, but crossing its mouth could see a long way up it. The scenery seemed to be of very much the same character as that we had left behind us in Dusky Sound.

We sailed to the north of and close to Breaksea Island, a hilly island of about 640 acres which lies opposite the entrance to the sound, and once more found ourselves out on the open sea.

It seemed almost a relief to get out into the open away from the shadow of the huge wall-like mountains, with their dark bushy sides, which had constantly hemmed us in for some time past. The complete freedom from sand-flies was also enjoyable. The sea was smooth, but as we got away from Breaksea Island we found a considerable roll setting in from the south-west. Indeed, this part of the ocean is never free from it, and one or two of our number were soon uncomfortable in consequence.

The day was an ideal one for a pleasure trip—a bright warm sun, and just fair breeze enough to keep our sails full. So we skimmed over the smooth blue water at the rate of about three knots an hour, helped not a little by the long following swell.

As far as could be seen, the coast line still preserved in the main the same appearance; bush-covered promontories standing out one behind the other, all much the same shape and slope, with indentations between them—too slight, however, to deserve the name of bays. The shore was fringed with a continuous line of foam, and dotted with reefs, isolated rocks, and small islands—some of the latter crowned with bush—and on them all flocks of penguins, shag, and gulls were to be seen basking in the sun. There may have been seals, too, but, although occasionally some one would say he could see one, they were never distinctly visible.

The mountains thus seen from a distance presented the appearance of a rampart of gigantic proportions running parallel to the coast, and rent asunder every few miles to form a sound. There were no rivers, only numerous cascades tumbling down through the bush to within a short distance of the sea. In many places the ocean rollers broke against the mountain sides; elsewhere the space between the bush and the sea was piled up with boulders. Sand was conspicuous by its absence. Above the 3,000 feet or so of the bush line appeared pile upon pile of rocky peaks, many of them capped with snow. At noon we were seven miles north of Breaksea Island, about one from shore, and opposite a cleft in the mountains, extending inland a few miles, which had the appearance of being a sound. I have no doubt it was one once, but it is now filled up, and a small creek called Coal River flows down the filled-up bed of the old sound, making, where it enters the sea, a small bar harbour workable with boats in fine weather. The bar is an accumulation of boulders and drift. A man named Brown, a native of Cod-Fish Island, is stated to be the author of a report that some Maories found coal there, and hence the name.

At 2.30 p.m. we were about fourteen miles north of Breaksea Island, and crossing the entrance to Dagg's Sound. This sound extends about eight miles in an east-south-east direction, and has a short arm going nearly due north near the head. Its depth is generally about 70 fathoms. The mountains about it are extremely precipitous, and the view as we sailed across its entrance was very fine. A large bluff, with luxuriant forest growth, projecting across and appearing to close the offing, had somewhat the appearance of a lion.

About two miles north of Dagg's Sound, shutting in and forming the head of a short narrow valley, we observed a high mountain, whose summit and sides, though not so steep as many of the adjacent ones, were, nevertheless, devoid of vegetation. The formation appeared to be nearly white, but what it was I am unable to say. The contrast this white mountain offered to the surrounding green heights was very remarkable. The breeze freshened as the day wore on, and we were soon off Doubtful Sound, 20 miles from Breaksea Island.

Doubtful Sound lies between the south coast of Secretary Island and the mainland, extends for about eight miles in an east-south-east direction, and then merges into Smith's Sound. The sound is about three miles wide for a distance of three miles from the mouth. There Banga Island, three miles long and one-and-a-half miles wide, is met with, the passage on either side of the island being not more than half-a-mile across. Seen from the sea, Banga Island appears to be the head of the sound, which thus has the appearance of being nothing more than an open bay.

At the south-east point of Secretary Island, where Doubtful Sound becomes Smith's Sound, Bradshaw's Sound penetrates the mainland in a north-easterly direction, and Thompson's Sound runs north-by-west between the east side of Secretary Island and the mainland.

Smith's Sound is but a continuation of Doubtful Sound, and and the two sounds together extend about twenty miles in an east-south-east direction. Three smaller sounds branch off from Smith's Sound in a south-west direction called First Arm, opposite Bradshaw's Sound; Crooked Arm, about half-way up; and Hall's Arm, at the head.

The scenery in all these sounds partakes of much the same type and is truly magnificent, especially that of Hall's Arm, which is considered by some to be superior to anything on the coast, not excepting Milford Sound. The head of Hall's Arm is, as I have said before, but three miles from the head of Breaksea Sound.

Bradshaw's Sound extends about seven miles in an east-north-east direction, and then branches into two arms, one—Precipice Cove—about two miles long to the north-north-east, and the other—Gaer Arm—extending some five miles to the south-east.

Thompson's Sound, which enters the sea nine miles to the north of Doubtful Sound, runs between the east coast of Secretary Island and the mainland. Secretary Island is triangular in shape, very mountainous, and covers about twenty-four square miles. It is, like the surrounding mountains, clothed with dense forests. The scenery about Doubtful Sound looked very rugged and grand as we sailed by on our course up the coast. It was the general opinion that it was the wildest we had yet seen. The afternoon was now well advanced, but the wind being fair and the weather fine we determined to make Thompson's Sound our next anchorage.

In 1887 I visited Doubtful Sound in the Government

steamer "Stella." We steamed right through the sound and out to sea by Thompson's Sound, thus going completely round Secretary Island. The scenery was splendid. The sound winds very much, and we ever seemed to be completely hemmed in by the land. The result was that we could never see much of the road we had come, or get but a circumscribed glimpse of the one we had yet to traverse.

We called on Mr. Seymour, a gentlemen who has determined to pass several years alone in this wild spot. He dwells by himself in a tent, with a dog or two, and is, I was told, studying the habits of the nocturnal birds of New Zealand, with the intention of writing a book about them. He had certainly chosen a romantic spot for his hermitage. His tent was pitched on the mainland, by the shore of a little bay; Secretary Island, with its varied outline of wooded mountains, and an intervening mile of water, constituting a glorious frontispiece. Behind and on both sides of Mr. Seymour's simple abode rose lofty green hills, and above them towered snow-covered peaks of giant proportions. A mountain torrent foamed into the little bay not many yards from his tent.

We arrived at the hermitage soon after sunrise one fine spring morning, and sent a boat off with stores for the hermit. He was an anxious-looking, middle-sized, middle-aged man. He said the rats on the mainland were destroying his stores, and accordingly he got the captain of the "Stella" to send a boat and shift his goods to a small island about two hundred yards from the shore. This island consisted of a few acres of rock covered with bush. Mr. Seymour had a small boat of his own, and I fancy he was searching for gold or other minerals, for among the stores we landed for him was a digger's cradle. We waited three hours for him to finish his correspondence, which consisted of seventeen letters for all parts of the world, the captain having previously had instructions from the Government to give the hermit every assistance. After getting his letters we steamed away, leaving him to his own society for another three months.

This man was once a school-master, holding a good position and moving in first-class society. He has renounced all these advantages for this solemn, solitary existence. As we steamed away, I saw him standing watching us from the shore. A group of sailors were near me looking at his solitary figure. "He won't see a soul for another three months now," said one, and then added reflectively and audibly "poor devil," a verdict generally endorsed by his hearers. The study of birds may have taken him there; but there are those who think—if not insanity—it is love that has induced this voluntary banishment from the abodes of men.

Again in 1888, one fine spring morning, we steamed into Thompson's Sound. Heavy masses of white mist rested here and there on the brows of the mountains, which, while partly hiding, yet at the same time enhanced the beauty of the scenery. One peculiarity of this sound consists in the numerous lovely valleys which branch from it at right angles. It has no islands to speak of, but the mountains on each side rise to between three and four thousand feet.

As we passed into Bradshaw's Sound the scenery grew wilder, and from there again we entered that splendid sheet of water known as Gaer Arm, and, steaming slowly up, anchored at its head. The views all round were superb; indeed, it is doubtful if it does not rival Milford. It certainly does in variety; but there are two or three views in Milford which may claim to be on a grander scale.

After a stay of a few hours we steamed back and out to sea by way of Doubtful Sound. The views on all sides were simply bewildering by reason of their number and their magnificence. Where all was so worthy of a lingering gaze, it was difficult to fix attention on any particular spot. Here we have a collection of sounds, all on view at the same time, each and all individually worthy of a long trip to enable one to satiate his appetite with the glories of their scenery. They do not possess the islands and hills of moderate elevation which we find mixed with views of more imposing grandeur in Dusky Sound, and which, to my mind, go far to make it the most enjoyable sound on the coast; but nowhere else will you come across such a group of sounds of the Milford type, all enclosed with huge mountains, as those which lie behind Secretary Island and are approached by Doubtful Sound from the south and Thompson's Sound from the north. On this second occasion we found that Mr. Seymour had grown tired of playing the hermit in Doubtful Sound, and had removed to the lighthouse settlement in Preservation Inlet.

On entering these sounds one thinks, as he proceeds up them, that nothing can be grander than the view he is looking at, and yet he has no doubt as he goes on that each view is finer than the last. As a matter of fact, the best views are generally obtained at the head.

A celebrated New Zealand photographer on entering Doubtful Sound was so convinced that nothing could be finer than the view he saw when but about a mile from the entrance, that he refused to go further. He was accordingly landed with his camera on a small island close at hand, and stayed there quite contented, while the steamer went on to the various arms, visiting of course infinitely more majestic scenery than that which had seemed to him incomparable and unsurpassable.

Passing through Thompson's Sound, the surface of the rocks in many places on both sides were seen to be worn quite smooth, probably the result of glacial action. At various points, too, they were marbled with viens of quartz. I also noticed masses of what appeared to be limestone on Secretary Island. Captain Fairchild, of the Government steamer, told me that pieces of obsidian had also been found on it. Secretary Island has evidently been cut off from the mainland, not unlikely by glacial action, Doubtful and Thompson's Sounds now filling the old glacier beds. In fact, all these sounds appear to me to have had this origin. The coast contiguous to the sounds follows a uniform straight line running nearly north-east, with scarcely any indentations of importance beyond the mouth of the sounds.

The sounds and their gorge-like valleys seemed carved out of a mass of the earth's crust rising abruptly from the coast line to an elevation of from 3,000 to close on 9,000 feet above sea level. This formation, which has in course of time been worn into the valleys and mountains we now behold, rises like a wall from out the ocean all along the coast from Preservation Inlet to Milford Sound (a distance of about 120 miles), and has its highest point not many miles inland. At Milford Sound it retires inland, forming a chain of mountains which, to the north of Milford, run parallel to the coast, but at a considerable distance from it, till they merge into the range of mountains known as the Southern Alps. The intervening stretch of country between these mountains and the sea is covered with lower elevations and terraces formed from drift brought down from the greater heights by glaciers and other denudiug forces of nature, which have been at work through countless ages. In this drift formation occur, as far as I have seen, all the gold fields as yet opened up on the West Coast, and it seems to be not improbable that the gold has been brought down from the back ranges. If my theory be correct, some day, I think, high up and deep in the masses of the Southern Alps and the lofty mountains which join them from the south, and which lie behind Jackson's and Big Bays, deposits of gold will be found compared to which all previous finds will be but as the reflected sunlight we receive from the moon is to the direct light of the sun at midday.

CHAPTER XI.

BUT to return to the "Rosa." After passing Doubtful Sound, we sailed pleasantly along the west of Secretary Island till we rounded its most northerly point, and found ourselves in the mouth of Thompson's Sound. We decided to put in here for the night, and at 5 p.m. we dropped anchor in a snug little harbour called Open Cove, about one-and-a-half miles from the entrance to the sound. Our day's sailing amounted to about 38 miles, and had been enjoyable in the extreme. Not only was the weather perfect, but the coast scenery had been grand, interesting, and unique.

Thompson's Sound is some 11 miles long, and generally about one wide. Its depth varies from 10 to 230 fathoms, and it averages about 130. Over 100 fathoms of water is also found far up both Smith's and Bradshaw's Sounds, 120 at the head of Precipice Cove, and 68 at that of Hall's Arm.

I have already referred to the scenery and formation of Thompson's Sound. The bay in which we were anchored had a boulder-strewn beach, and the skipper, self, and some others landed with our tools, and started prospecting; but the sand-flies came in such swarms and were so ferociously blood-thirsty that our powers of endurance gave way, and gathering up our tools we absolutely fled to the boat and returned to the cutter. They were soon swarming there, and quite thick in the cabin; but from that sanctum we speedily ousted them by starting smoking. The only thing in the way of minerals we found on shore were specimens of fine white marble.

We left Open Cove next morning at half-past four, and, standing out to sea, continued our voyage up the coast in beautiful weather, and with a fair wind and smooth sea. At 7 a.m. we were off Nancy Sound, and half-an-hour later were close to Charles Sound, the many pointed peaks of Mount Paulina—a lofty mountain a little to the south of Caswell's Sound—forming a conspicuous object in the view ahead of us.

Nancy and Charles Sounds are two small sounds, each about eight miles long, and have soundings of over 100 fathoms. They extend in a south-east direction. Nancy is four and Charles eight miles from Thompson's Sound. Charles Sound has an arm branching to the east about five miles from the sea. This arm is called Emelius, and is about three miles long. Fort Arm at the head of Nancy's is some one-and-a-half miles long, and bears to the north-east. Charles Sound has the reputation of being a good sealing ground. On the face of one of the mountains near its head there crops out a considerable deposit of marble. The position of this marble could be seen from the cutter. Pat, who had visited it, told me it was white in colour, and seemed to be of good quality. Hitherto all the sounds we had seen had much the same appearance, and seemed to be of the same formation. There were no beaches, except small ones at the foot of cascades, formed by the *débris* brought down by the rushing torrents. At the head of the sounds are alluvial swampy flats packed with snags.

As we neared Caswell's Sound, we noticed just to the south of it several beaches and small terraces behind them. This struck me as being a not unlikely looking spot to find gold, if there was any about, but as yet all our efforts to find any trace of the precious metal in the sounds had failed; and, except at Preservation Inlet, I have not heard of anybody finding it in this region. At all events we have no reliable reports on the subject. I have often been told that men have found gold in this or that sound, but they never bring it away with them ; and, what is more, they don't go back to look for it. We came to the conclusion that it is unlikely gold exists in the the sounds south of Milford. We found no trace of it, either free or in rocks ; but then the country is so precipitous and so covered with bush that prospecting it must be a matter of many years to come before anyone can state at all positively that payable gold does not exist. We were opposite to the entrance of Caswell's Sound at half-past eight, and the view was very fine. The snow-capped Mary Peaks, nearly 6,000 feet high, about 12 miles off and situate near its head, formed a magnificent back-ground to the sound which stretched before us, with its adjacent giant mountains, among which Mount Paulina, close at hand, and 4,200 feet high, towered majestically.

Caswell's Sound is about ten miles long, and thirteen miles north of Thompson's. It extends in an east-south-east direction, and is generally about 100 fathoms deep. The surrounding mountains are very lofty. Just at the entrance it is not more than 800 yards wide, but soon opens out to more than two miles, and narrows down again to about half-a-mile at the head. Gold is said to have been found on its shores in places, as well as large deposits of white marble. The latter has been worked at various times and a good deal of money spent in the experiment, but nothing has come of it, and, for the present at all events, operations have ceased. The marble is nearly a pure white in colour, and I have seen several specimens of it manufactured into vases and other ornaments, which undoubtedly had a handsome appearance. It does not, however, seem to exist in large pieces. The whole deposit appears to have been shaken—perhaps by an earthquake—and to be cracked all through, so that when quarried it comes away in fragments.

After passing Caswell's Sound, the coast-line for some distance became less rugged, the immediate mountains lower, and in many places extensive flat-topped terraces of a moderate elevation were observed. These terraces, so far as I could judge, were composed of drift and gravel, and may possibly in the future become gold fields of a limited extent.

Three miles from Caswell's, we passed Tom Thumb Bay, a small bay with a reef of rocks outside and said to be a fair boat harbour.

Four miles further on we sailed past Looking-glass Bay. This bay is about a mile deep and half-a-mile wide at the mouth, and has the appearance of being the entrance of a sound. It is a fair harbour when the wind does not come from the north-west. There is a good deal of terrace formation and comparatively level land around its shores, and gold is reported to have been found in the neighbourhood.

About four miles north of Looking-glass Bay, we passed close to House-roof Rock, a huge isolated rock rising out of the water about 400 yards from the shore. The top is shaped not unlike the roof of a house, and its general appearance strongly reminds one of a Noah's Ark. There are a few shrubs growing on the rock.

At about half-past ten we opened up George Sound, having covered a distance of 28 miles since we left Thompson's Sound at half past four.

From Caswell's to a few miles beyond George Sound we passed a succession of terraces, not by any means an unfavourable spot for gold prospecting.

The best way to work this part of the coast would be to take a cutter into George or Caswell's Sounds, and land with tent, stores, tools, &c., in a whale-boat at various points. Such a plan of operations could be easily carried out in fine weather.

George Sound extends in a south-south-east direction, and is 12 miles long. A considerable stream flows into its head. About a mile up this stream is a small lake, the head of which is said to be only two miles distant from the Poseidon River which flows into Milford Sound.

George Sound is rather an open one. Its depth varies from 30 to 100 fathoms. It is surrounded by lofty mountains, its head waters being overshadowed by peaks of from 5,000 to 7,000 feet elevation.

I think a tolerably easy road could be made from the head of this sound to the Poseidon River, and down the side of the river to Milford Sound. If this were done, it would give the tourist the most get-at-able and magnificent piece of mountain travelling in New Zealand. The trip would be by steamer to the head of George Sound—which in itself is well worth coming a long way to see—and thence by ponies or on foot to the head of Milford Sound.

The scenery down the Poseidon is truly marvellous. The

Sutherland Falls, near its head waters, are said by those who have seen them to surpass in altitude and sublimity anything of the kind in the world. The river is about 25 miles long from its rise to where it enters Milford Sound.

About nine miles from the sound it enters Lake Ada, a narrow sheet of water five miles long and surrounded by the grandest mountain scenery. Taking the nearest point of contact, the distance from Lake Ada to Milford Sound is four miles. The scenic beauties of the sound, I need hardly remind my readers, are well-known and far-famed. The traveller could break his journey at the falls, and amuse himself fishing, fern gathering, or mountaineering. Trout have been put into the Poseidon, and if they flourish as they have done elsewhere in New Zealand, the efforts of the angler will soon be rewarded with the capture of monsters of 10 lbs., 20 lbs., and even 30 lbs. weight.

While on this subject I should like to express my firm conviction that if the introduction of salmon to New Zealand waters is ever to be successfully carried out, the young fry must be turned into such places as Lake Ada or Lake McKerrow near Martin's Bay, and similar lakes on the West Coast, and not into the unsuitable rivers of the south and east coast where efforts have hitherto been unsuccessfully made to rear them. I think myself it is a pity that trout should have been turned into such a likely salmon river as the Poseidon, for they will certainly play havoc with young salmon, and be an impediment to the eventual introduction of the king of fish. Where the salmon successfully acclimatised on the West Coast, it could not fail to be a source of great wealth to the country. Stock the West Coast Sounds with salmon, and I do not doubt that this would attract a considerable population in the course of time. Then by degrees we should witness the development of the rich mineral resources which it is almost certain are hidden in the recesses of the gigantic forest-covered mountain ranges which I have so often described.

A sail of six miles from George Sound brought us to the mouth of Bligh Sound. As we approached this sound the mountains again rose abruptly from the sea, being very lofty, with many snow-capped peaks. I noticed during this voyage that snow was generally an indication of an elevation of about 5,000 feet. An excellent view of the rugged heights of Mount Longsight, 4,800 feet, the Hawrenny Peaks,

6,500 feet, and the Mitre Peaks, 5,500 (the latter in the
distance) affording ample . satisfaction to those who take
any pleasure in seeing how un-get-at-able this earth of ours
can be. The mountains, though higher, shewed much less
rock on the surface than had been the case further south, and
revealed traces of numerous and frequent landslips. As we
opened up Bligh Sound the view was very fine. Mount Longsight, which rises abruptly from the sea and forms the northern
boundary of the sound for many miles, impressed everybody. The peaks of the huge mountains which are about
Milford were also at this point prominent features in the landscape.

Bligh Sound extends in a south-east direction about five
miles, then turns sharply to the right and keeps south-west
for the next five; turns again to the left, and continues south-
east for three miles, when the head is reached. This zig-zag
contour can be traced in many of the sounds and inland lakes
of the South Island, and is probably the course cut by ancient
glaciers out of the surrounding elevated country. The general
depth of Bligh Sound varies from 40 to 78 fathoms. There is
a harbour at the head of the sound called Bounty Haven,
where bottom is found at seven fathoms. The mountains
about this sound are rugged and steep, and at its head are a
pile of snow-clad giants running up to 7,000 feet. It is
amongst these that the river Poseidon rises, the river being at
its nearest point about four miles from the head of the sound.

We did not go into Bligh Sound, but continued our course
towards Milford. Three miles from Bligh Sound we passed
Little Bay, an indentation in the coast line shut in by steep
snow-crowned mountains between 5,000 and 6,000 feet high.
There are some remarkable-looking rocks at the south end of
the bay, which is said to be a tolerably safe harbour for small
craft in southerly weather.

Five miles more and we came to Poison Bay. This bay
is reputed to be a good haven of safety in most winds. There
is a deep gorge-like valley behind it, which appears to be the
mouth of a filled-up sound.

Once when passing Poison Bay in a steamer, the Captain
said to me, " Ah, Poison Bay ought to have been a sound,
only Dr. ——'s ice melted before he finished it." (Dr. —— is
a well-known but dogmatic geologist). " That man talks, not
only as if he knew all about how the world was made, but as

if he helped to make it. I had him round with me one trip. He knew everything, and shewed how this part of the world had been made, and I guess he could tell you how many tons of ice it took to cut out each of the sounds. He's not always right though. Once he wrote a paper proving that no gold would ever be found in a certain locality; but, as it happened, very rich gold was found in that locality, and thereupon Dr. —— immediately wrote another paper in which he ignored his first, and shewed not only that the gold was there, but how it came there, and how he knew it ought to be there. He did exactly the same about some coal deposits on the West Coast. First of all he wrote a paper asserting their was no coal worth speaking about in the locality indicated, and then, when big seams were found, he wrote another paper shewing when the coal was put there, and why it was put there."

When off Poison Bay, Mount Pembroke, 6,800 feet high and one of the mountains about Milford Sound, presented a grand appearance. Just at this time patches of feathery white mist made their appearance on many of the higher peaks, and the mixture of snow, black rocks, and sun-gilded mist made a very imposing picture.

A little gold has been obtained about Poison Bay. It suffers, in reputation at all events, from one very serious drawback—viz., its atmosphere is said to be darkened with sand-flies.

Sailing pleasantly along another seven miles brought us to Milford Sound; but long before we entered Milford we could make out away to the north the south point of Big Bay, and at last saw before us the terminating point of our voyage in the "Rosa." All were happy at the thought of soon being ashore, for the voyage—all huddled together as we were, twelve men with not accommodation for six—was not improving our tempers. Quarrels had also taken place between our Danes and the sailors, the hot-tempered skipper in particular seeming to be very much down on the Dutchmen, as he called them. A fortnight had been the time estimated to suffice to bring us from the Bluff to Big Bay, and now the end of four weeks found us still on the voyage.

CHAPTER XII.

WE entered Milford Sound at 3 p.m., having sailed 50 miles since we left Thompson's at half-past four, and a delightful sail it had been in all truth. Between Bligh and Milford the views looking landward had been sublime. Panorama succeeded panorama, each seeming more magnificent than the preceding one. And, indeed, this was the case, for, as we neared Milford, peaks of 6,000, 7,000, 8,000, and one of 9,000 feet elevation came in view. It was evident as we entered Milford that to the north of the sound the high mountains retired inland, a series of beaches, terraces and hills of moderate elevation stretching along the coast as far as eye could see.

On entering the sound, to the left Mount Pembroke rose majestically from the sea to a height of nearly 7,000 feet, its numerous peaks capped with snow, and its steep sides luxuriating in rich forest growth for fully 3,000 feet above sea level. In front of us the mountains came down to the water like sheer walls, their sides apparently absolutely perpendicular. They seemed to meet about two miles from us, and one could hardly conceive that there was any passage between them; they seemed, indeed, to bar our further progress. To the right rose forest-clad hills, above whose dark-green crests

towered the castellated points of Mitre Peak, the most strikingly shaped mountain in New Zealand. Numerous photo-
graphs have been taken of this remarkable formation, and can
be obtained in nearly every large centre of British civilisation.

We passed St. Ann's Point, a low projecting ridge of bare
rocks off the south entrance, and sailing round it about half-
a-mile found ourselves in a snug little harbour encircled with
wooded hills, called Anita Bay, where we anchored. I immediately had the whale-boat lowered, and with a party of four
started for a pull up the sound.

At Anita Bay the sound is about two miles wide; two
miles further on, at Dale Point, it is only 500 yards, with the
water 60 fathoms deep, and perpendicular cliffs about 4,000
feet high overhanging us on either side. You can, therefore,
imagine something of the scenery we had in view as, on this
summer afternoon, over still water, we pulled our boat up the
far-famed Milford Sound. To the left was Mount Pembroke,
6,800 feet; to the right, the tops of Mitre and Hawrenny
Peaks, 5,500 feet, could be seen projecting above the huge
green walls which rose from the waters of the sound; in
front the 4,000 feet cliffs seemed to meet, and, as I have just
before observed, render further progress impossible

· We found a considerable swell coming in from the sea as
we pulled out of Anita Bay, but it diminished as we progressed, and by the time we reached Dale Point it had died
away.

For two miles from this point there was nothing to be seen
but two huge green walls on each side of us, with streams of
water here and there tumbling down them. Keeping close to
the left wall, we could see the points of Mitre Peak above the
right one.

Getting through the narrows the sound opened out, and
rounding a point there suddenly burst upon us, as if by magic,
perhaps the most marvellous vision of scenic grandeur to be
found on the West Coast of New Zealand, if not in the whole
world. Maybe the observer is more struck with it on account
of the suddenness with which it bursts upon his astonished
gaze, and it is on that account I am inclined to rank it before
all other views. We stopped rowing as if by instinct, and for
a time looked on in silent rapture upon this wondrous vista
of beauty. It was some minutes before the dead silence was
broken by any of the crew.

H.

We were but a few yards from Stirling Waterfall, a magnificent cascade of great volume, which, emanating from the snows of Mount Pembroke, here precipitates itself in a few falls—the lowest of which is close on 1,000 feet—over the left wall into the waters of the sound.

We regarded this splendid fall and the dark gorge we had come through for some time with intense admiration. We were so close to the base of the huge cliff it tumbles over, that the fall appeared to be hanging over us. The top of the cliff could not be seen ; it seemed, indeed, to pierce the sky. Next turning round, before us stretched the upper waters of Milford Sound, still as a millpond, and from two to three miles wide, with the outlines of the stupendous mountains reflected on their surface. We were about five miles from the head, but it hardly looked one, and the Bowen Falls, four miles distant, seemed close at hand. Time did not permit us to advance just then any further into fairyland, and so we pulled back to the cutter.

Going through the narrows we met a strong head wind, and had rather a hard pull for about an hour; but once past Dale Point the breeze died away, and we rowed into Anita Bay over a glassy sea lighted with the reflection of a gorgeous sunset, and heaving to the dying pulse of the distant ocean.

It was dark when we got on board. As I smoked a pipe on deck before turning in I could hear the moan of the waves as they broke at the entrance to the sound, while the cry of the penguins from all sides mingled with the voice of the land birds. I felt that I had just seen a piece of indescribably grand scenery. To try to imagine an increase of grandeur would be, as I think Dr. Johnson somewhere remarks, " ridiculous because impossible."

M., who had been on shore at Anita Bay, gave me some small water-worn pieces of greenstone he had picked up. The stone was transparent and of a pea-green colour, an indifferent quality of the greenstone found at various places on the West Coast, though much valued by the Maories, who worked it into ornaments and weapons before they acquired the manners of the Pakeha. It takes a fine polish, and is now a good deal used for watch chains and other ornaments. Its technical name is nephrite, a kind of tremolite, a variety of hornblende ; an anhydrous silicate, composed of silica and magnesia with little or no iron, commonly called jade. It occurs usually in association with talcose or magnesian rocks. It is also found in China, Mexico, and Peru. The Spaniards discovered many ornaments carved from this stone in the possession of the Mexicans and Peruvians when they first landed in those countries in the good old days, and brought the people within the fold of the Christian Church by rooting out and extirpating the population for the glory and honour of his Most Christian Majesty of Spain. There are various varieties of jade on the West Coast, some so fibrous in structure that it might almost be called asbestos; color pale green, and easily split into stiff, brittle fibres. In this form it occurs in enormous deposits, but it does not appear to have any commercial value, being too brittle to either polish like greenstone or work up like asbestos. I have seen specimens of what might be called all the transition forms from jade to asbestos. The stone at Anita Bay is hard and compact enough to take a good polish. There is a quarry of it on the face of a hill just above the bay which appears to have been worked at some time or other. Pat said that the Maories used in years past to come regularly to Anita Bay for the stone.

The night turned dull and cloudy, with fitful gusts of wind blowing up the sound, and so strong that we congratulated ourselves on having turned back in the whale-boat when we did. Had we have delayed much longer it is doubtful if we could have got back to the cutter at all that night.

All next day (December 1st) was wet, with a heavy north-west gale, and we did nothing. The second was fine, though a heavy south-west gale was blowing, and a big sea running outside.

As the weather seemed broken and there was no chance of being able to put to sea for a day or two at least, we decided to cut a track through the bush to Transit Beach.

Transit Beach is about three miles to the south of St. Ann's Point. Pat said he had heard there was gold there. About three in the afternoon all hands landed, and we made a start.

I could see from the cutter that there was a saddle between the hills, bearing 280° by my prismatic compass, and as by the chart Transit Beach was in about the same direction, I decided to cut the track on that bearing.

We had far more men than were needed for cutting one track, for as the track was but four feet wide two men would have been ample—one with a slasher for the small growth going first, and the other man armed with an axe following and cutting the heavy stuff. Instead of two we were eleven strong, armed with slashers and billhooks for cutting the undergrowth and small timber and axes for felling such trees as might impede our progress.

The country was covered with the usual dense forest, chiefly birch, with a few red pines and fuchsia trees and a thick growth of ferns and creepers, chief among the latter being the gee-gee and supple-jack.

The gee-gee is a very handsome creeper; its leaves, which are like sword blades in shape, grow in crowns and branch from the main vine every foot or so. The vine is generally two or three inches in diameter, and the crowns often two or three feet across. I have seen these gee-gee vines climbing 60 feet and more up a tree, and completely hiding its trunk with their graceful plumes. The blossom is in long, white, feathery flowers, and the fruit is juicy and wholesome.

Creepers, ferns, and small trees rapidly disappeared before our men, everything being cut close to the ground, and soft places bridged over. The track was made serviceable for the transit of loads in case our discoveries at Transit Beach made it worth while camping there for any time.

The *modus operandi* was thus:—I, with the compass, went first, taking two men with me, and pushed my way through the bush, keeping the line by the compass as far as the men behind could conveniently see or hear me. I then stood still and they commenced to cut in the direction where I had come to a halt. The two men with me meanwhile pushed on as far as I could see them, or made for any conspicuous mark which might be in the line. They would next turn and commence cutting towards me. Then, when the two cutting parties had nearly met, I would move on, taking the first two with me, and the operation described above would be repeated. Most of my time was thus occupied in standing still with the compass in my hands. The sand-flies took a mean advantage of my position, especially when I was taking bearings, and could not brush them away. The men at work escaped this martyrdom, as they are slow-moving brutes, and do not settle on you till you have been standing still a second or two. This was the first time I had seen the whole party at work; some of them I noticed did not shape very well, and seemed to have very vague ideas as to when they were in the line or cutting in the right direction. Old Julius, as we now called him, worked splendidly, and shewed himself an experienced bushman. When he was once started he kept the line like a bee, and laid about him with a heavy slasher in most effectual style. The other men said they could do most work with tools as light as possible, but Julius, on the contrary, claimed to be able to do more work and to feel less tired if he used tools of a good weight ; .and, provided a man knows how to use them, I believe old Julius to be right. But with amateurs, as a rule, the lighter their tools the better.

The ground, as we proceeded, was undulating and rising. We crossed several small gullies with running water in them. It was probably the creek which enters Anita Bay, close to where we had started our track, crossing and re-crossing our path. The creek bed was everywhere spangled with glistening yellow mica. Having cut about 50 chains of track we returned to the cutter at nightfall.

Early next morning we resumed operations, and soon found ourselves in a swampy flat which was covered with stunted trees and a thick undergrowth of flax, reeds, and gee-gee. I sent a man up a tree to have a look-out, and he reported high land on both sides, but not in front. From this I concluded we were on top of the saddle seen from the cutter. We were now about 200 feet above the sea level according to the barometer. We cut our way across the flats—very swampy and flat—for about a mile, and then the ground began to fall rapidly, and we were soon in thick forest again. Before long we could hear the waves breaking on Transit Beach below us. Cutting about 30 chains after leaving the flat brought us to a dense growth of tutu and veronica, which more or less all along the coast exposed to the open sea makes a thick fringe between the bush proper and high water mark.

The veronica creeps right down to high-water mark, its roots inserting themselves between and into any crevices that may occur in rock or boulder. I have often seen big rocks and boulders surrounded by water at high tide, and apparently devoid of soil, with their tops covered with a cluster of bright veronica. In stormy days, too, I have again and again noticed the waves washing into the veronica fringe. This variety of veronica has a large leaf, pink flower, grows about 14 feet high, and is very valuable for making breakwinds to gardens,

&c., especially near the sea.   It grows very fast when planted out, and makes a handsome evergreen hedge.

Cutting through the fringe we found ourselves on Transit Beach at about half-past ten, and saw on all sides a rock-bound coast strewn with granite, schist, and a few white marble boulders.   I came upon a rugged fragment of iron ore, about two feet through each way.   It had much the appearance of some iron ore I have seen from the West of Scotland.   Old Julius told me he had once worked at some iron works in Sweden, and the ore used exactly resembled this fragment. We set to work prospecting, but found no gold.   There was, however, plenty of yellow mica, with which, indeed, the whole country seems to be peppered.   The sand-flies came in millions, and we presently determined it was not worth while staying any longer, and so returned forthwith to Anita Bay.   It was a warm afternoon, and when I got back to the bay I sent my garments off to the cutter in one of the boats, and then swam off myself, having a delicious swim of about 200 yards.

Next morning at sunrise we weighed anchor, some of us being so sanguine of being landed at Big Bay before night as to do up swags and get all ready for going ashore.   We stood out of Milford with a light, fair breeze, but it died away as the sun got up.   Then the sky began to get dirty to the north-west, with a falling glass, so we turned after a couple of hours and took up our old quarters at Anita Bay.

The storm came on at 11 a.m., with very heavy rain, and the rest of the day was spent in idling, smoking, yarning, playing cards, and fishing.   C. and I in the cabin tested some of the stones we had found at different places, and for this purpose had recourse to acids and blow-pipe.   There was no doubt about the presence of plenty of iron in them all, and little else; one specimen though indicated faint traces of nicol.

The fishermen caught a few dozen crayfish, a blind eel, a few cod, a groper three feet, and a shark four feet long.   The crayfish were caught in a roughly constructed pot.   They can be caught here and at many other places on the New Zealand coast by the ton.   Often when net fishing I have seen them clustering on the net in dozens, and eating what fish there might be in it, but the brutes always dropped off and escaped as the net was being hauled in.   In some places, if we left our nets down an hour or two, we would be pretty sure to find the fish all more or less eaten by crayfish, with nothing but the heads and back bones left in many instances. They are about as large as a lobster in the body, but want the two large claws. Many people consider them equal and even superior to the lobster for the table, but I cannot say that I endorse that opinion. I have always found them very insipid by comparison.

The blind eel is an abominable creator of nastiness, in a mass of which it lives. It envelopes itself in a bag of the most filthy-looking, evil-smelling slime imaginable, and makes a horrible mess of anything it comes in contact with. For my part I would prefer to cut the line and let a blind eel away with the hook sooner than have anything to do with it. As far as I have seen they are generally about 2 feet long, not unlike a thick fresh-water eel to look at.

Sharks are said to swarm on this coast, but I never saw any ; and when the water is still, as it often was, one generally sees their black back fin shewing above the surface if there are any big ones about. The one caught by our man had a mouth large enough to enable it to give a severe bite.

CHAPTER XIII.

THE next two days were pouring wet and very windy, so
that we were mostly confined to the cutter. Things did
not go very pleasantly, for the Captain showed a good deal of
nasty temper. He seems to have a great aversion to the
Danes, and for little or no reason flies down their throats.
His tongue is as sharp as a two-edged sword, while his language would most certainly class A1 at Billingsgate. The
Danes seem thoroughly cowed by this black-browed, salt-
skinned savage. He is very civil to me, but I shall be glad
to be landed at Big Bay and clear of him and his cutter. He
is, however, a very able seaman.

Next morning, the 7th of December, was dull, with a little
rain and light wind, but a heavy sea running from the west
made it useless to try Big Bay, as, had we gone, there would
have been too much surf to allow us to land. We went on
shore and again prospected, and found small pieces of fine
white marble and good greenstone and also huge masses of
inferior greenstone. Next we sunk a shaft, went through a
bed of blue pipe-clay, and got into a drift of mullock and iron-

stained earth and granite boulders. There were no traces of gold or even black sand; plenty of sand composed of garnets and stained quartz—called ruby sand—was discovered by the men. Found a large schapper lying on the beach not quite dead. This is one of the best eating of the New Zealand fish, but chiefly confined to the North Island, and I never heard of one so far south before.

On the 8th there was a tremendous downpour all day. I obtained a first-class shower bath by standing undressed on the deck for two or three minutes. In the cabin everything was wet—floor soaking, walls running, and ceiling dripping. Throughout the whole day there was a roar all round of thundering cataracts, both close at hand and miles away, and the furious torrent of rain that pelted down covered the sea with large bubbles. We made a guage of a common bucket, and, calculating the amount that fell, found it came to 20 inches between 8 a.m. and 6 p.m.

At 9 p.m. I was standing on the deck in my oilskins, the night being pitch dark and the rain still descending in a perfect deluge, when suddenly we were startled by a tremendous report, which continued like heavy thunder for 10 seconds, and which seemed to make the cutter tremble. Some said it was an earthquake and spoke of the chances of a tidal wave following, but most of us considered it to be a landslip. One man declared that if it was a landslip it must have been half a mountain that tumbled down, and further, that if it had fallen into the water we should have a tremendous wave upon us in a minute. However, nothing of the kind occurred, and we passed the night in peace, our chief trouble being to arrange oilskins and waterproof sheeting in such a manner as to keep the numerous drips from the cabin ceiling off our blankets. Fleas were now swarming, and a tin of insecticide C. had brought with him came in very useful.

Next morning broke extremely fine, not a cloud in the sky. The landslip we had heard during the night could now be clearly seen, extending along the side of a mountain for about two miles at about 800 feet above the sea, and not more than a mile from where we lay at anchor. Every one landed and proceeded to inspect the slip. We found from the direction of the landslip that the flood had cut a gut 20 feet deep and half a chain in width through the bush, carrying trees, bush, rocks, and boulders before its impetuous torrent and piling them up in a huge mound many feet high and fully three chains broad on the sea beach close to where we had commenced the track to Transit Beach. We prospected up this gut; as we ascended we got some fine views of Mount Pembroke, and could see the slip above us to the left. We at last came upon it at the end of the channel about one mile from the beach. We then found ourselves under a newly formed cliff with a face several hundred feet high, over which tumbled two cascades. This was the commencement of the slip at the greatest distance from the sea, and it was evident that a good deal of the *débris* brought away by it had been washed down the gut and helped to form the heap on the beach. This gut, if it were kept clear, would constitute a nice trip for tourists visiting Milford Sound, for it affords a ready means of penetrating into the New Zealand bush not often met with in the sounds. There is beautiful forest on each side full of vines, creepers, and ferns, among the latter being the gigantic mummock, whose fronds not unfrequently measure as much as 16 feet in length.

In the bed of the gut were boulders of granite containing small lodes of garnet, reefs of what looked like granitic gneiss displaying veins of marble in profusion, and large pieces of pure white marble. One in particular, four feet long, three feet deep, and 14 inches thick had evidently been broken off a reef. There were also masses of slag and hornblende. The ground where the water had been running and subsided, as well as the bed of the creek which flowed down the channel, positively glittered with yellow and silver mica. Some of the former looked wonderfully like gold; so much so that one of the men seeing a crevice in a rock full of it, declared it was and must be gold. He accordingly proceeded to dig some out with his knife, and then pronounced it to be mica, but found consolation in the observation that gold couldn't look any different. We also came across a little iron pyrites, but no trace of gold or black sand was to be seen. We, however, did not waste our time; we had three guns with us and shot twenty-four kakas and some pigeons.

The day was beautiful all through; the air after the rain was fresh and delicious, and, above all, till towards evening, there was scarcely a sandfly to bother us. This was, indeed, a relief.

We returned to the cutter in the evening, everybody in a

good humour. Pieces of mummock were brought away for cooking purposes, but though the Maories are said to prize it highly I cannot say that our party appreciated it much.

The warm sun had dried up everything, and the change from the constant drip and damp of the last two days was agreeable in the extreme.

Next morning, the 10th of December, we weighed anchor at eight o'clock, and, there being but little wind, stood out to sea. The dog Jack, a large brown retriever good for nothing but eating and swimming, was left behind. A day or two before some of the men had gone round the Point in a boat and taken Jack with them. They pulled about three miles from Anita, landed, shot a few birds, and went back to their boat ; but Jack refused to come with them, and they left him to his fate. They said that owing to the nature of the coast it was impossible he could make his way along the beach to Anita Bay, while he was not likely to find it through the bush. The little terrier, Fan, bought by M. in Dunedin, had by this time taken a great fancy to myself, and would follow no one else. She had evidently been a great pet, and knew a lot of tricks. She was dainty at first, turning up her nose at porridge and fish, but hunger soon taught her the necessity of eating all she could get of any kind.

While at Anita Bay one day I, in wandering over the rocks which stretch for some distance behind St. Ann's Point, came upon several impressions in the hard granite rock as of human feet—for all the world as if someone with boots on had been walking on the rocks when they were soft. Some of the imprints were such as would be made by a three-year-old child, others by a full-grown man. A better and more distinct impression of footprints could not well be.

As we got out of the sound the wind fell away, and we met a heavy swell rolling in from the west, so heavy as to put all ideas of landing at Big Bay out of the question. The glass commenced to fall, too, so we turned round, and re-entering Milford ran right up to the head of the sound, and there anchored in Freshwater Basin, just in front of Sutherland's house and half-a-mile above Bowen Falls. The wind freshened as we got into the sound, and we had half a gale behind us when passing through the narrows. We ran aground in Freshwater Basin, but hauled off with a kedge, and dropped anchor. Since we have been in Milford it has blown a gale of more or less violence through the narrows every day, generally up it, no matter what the weather might be outside.

Milford Sound is about nine miles long, and after passing Sterling Falls, which are about half-way up, and which we visited in the whale-boat on the first night of our arrival at Milford, the scenery grows more and more imposing until a glorious, stupendous, bewildering climax is reached at the head of the sound.

From our anchorage we had in prospect, looking from north to east, a stretch of the sound with the huge walls of rock rising 4,000 feet from the water's edge; snow-clad Pembroke 6,800, and Tutako 9,000 feet in the background; and the magnificent Bowen Falls near at hand. From east to south we commanded a view of Sutherland's house, with a 5,000-feet hill behind it, and 7,000-feet peaks behind that; the valley of the Cleddaw; a portion of Sheerdown Range (about 5,000 feet high), and Deep Water Basin

From south to west we had Deep Water Basin, Sheerdown Range, the valley of Lake Ada, and the Poseidon River, with a background of lofty mountains. From west to north—perhaps the best view of all—we beheld a stretch of water, still, and reflecting with mirror-like fidelity on its calm and placid surface the glorious panorama of mountain and forest shadowed in its clear depths. Beyond this scene of sweet tranquility rose those wonderful ranges of highlands of which Hawrenny and Mitre Peaks are the highest points. These ranges are exceptionally precipitous in their outline, and terminate in sharp teeth-like peaks, Mitre Peak being perhaps the sharpest.

We were anchored half-a-mile away from Bowen Falls, yet the air was filled with spray from it, making the decks and everything wet.

Mr. Sutherland, whose house we could see not far off, is a man who has spent several years in this intensely lovely solitude. He is said to be looking for minerals, somewhat after the style of Docherty at Dusky Sound, every now and again turning up at Wellington or Dunedin with specimens and reports of valuable discoveries, though as yet nothing has come of them. He is a tall, heavily-built man, with fresh complexion and bright blue eyes, and is likely to go down to posterity as the discoverer of the great waterfall which bears his name. I fancy that by degrees history will convert him into a hero, although I do not know that there is anything especially heroic in living in a comfortable house in the midst of such glorious scenery, with a Government steamer waiting on him every three months, and several other steamers calling during the year, obtaining a free passage to Wellington or Dunedin whenever he wants one, and then staying a month or two in town getting money for shares in his discoveries and receiving help to enable him to open up the country.

I heard from very good authority that Sutherland once got £40 to commence cutting a track from Milford to Wakalipu Lake, he having reported that he had found a very good one with a saddle only 200 or 300 feet high. The city fathers of Queenstown (the capital of the Wakalipu district) who voted him this money, then began to think that Wakalipu was itself a thousand feet above Milford, and that there must be something wrong about the 200 feet saddle. Accordingly they declined to send Sutherland any more money, and the track was never cut. As far as I can see he has done nothing to speak of yet for the time he has been here. There was a standing offer of £300 to anyone who would find a decent track over the mountains from the West Coast Sounds to the interior. Such a track was recently found by a young surveyor named M'Kinnon, who came through to Milford from Te Anau Lake on the other side. Sutherland now says he could have found the track at any time if he had wanted to do so.

Recently he went to Dunedin with some very good specimens of rough gold which he represented he had got out of a claim he was working to the north of Milford Sound. Several men were induced by him to pay for a share in the claim. One man to my knowledge paid £75 sterling, and I don't know what the others gave him, but when they got to the place where Sutherland had told them they would make their fortunes, they found one little patch of gold and no more. Four of them named Brebner, Richardson, Woolfe, and Perry left Sutherland in disgust, and, getting a boat, went prospecting up the coast to the north. The poor fellows had their boat upset in going into the river at Martin's Bay, and were all drowned in November, 1887. Two of my men helped to bury them at Martin's Bay some weeks after the accident.

A gentleman who has known Sutherland for years told me that Sutherland also came to him with the sample of gold he took to Dunedin, and by means of which he enticed the men to purchase shares in the claim. As soon as he saw the gold the gentleman in question remarked, " Very pretty nuggets Mr. Sutherland, very pretty ; I remember them perfectly well ; you showed them to me just five years ago." Sutherland did business elsewhere after that pointed rebuff.

That Sutherland is a man of taste is evident to any one who has been in his house, while his surveys of the district show considerable ability in one who has not been trained to the work.

Before long I have no doubt there will be an hotel at Lake Ada or Sutherland's Falls. Possibly the hotel would do best at the head of the sound, somewhere near where Sutherland himself is, with accommodation houses at the other places of interest. Sutherland will most likely be the landlord, and with his hotel and boats and guides to the mountains, should make a good thing of the enterprise. I have no doubt, at all events, that he will be regarded by the tourists, who are almost certain to come here in large numbers, as one of the wonders of New Zealand, and further, I should say, he will deserve his honours and prosperity as much as most people who draw prizes in life's lottery. Everything comes to him who waits, and Sutherland, if he has done nothing else, has certainly waited long at Milford Sound.

It is curious, by the way, how these hermit-like men dislike each other. Docherty was once a passenger, with Sutherland, by the Government steamer. After Sutherland had been landed at Milford, Docherty turned to the Captain and said, " You would observe, Captain, that I did not speak to Sutherland ; I am a worker ; I have nothing to do with a loafer like him." I have heard, too, that Sutherland says as much for Docherty.

Another hermit, called Maori Bill, who has spent more than twenty years, mostly by himself, in the bush, living on roots and what birds his dogs could catch for him, once met Docherty on board a West-Coast steamer, and said, " How do you do Mr. Docherty ? " " You have the advantage of me," replied Docherty, either not knowing or pretending not to know him. " So has anyone who has a little common sense," came Maori Bill's spiteful retort.

If there are only two or three settlers together they generally manage to fall out. Many years ago I went overland from Queenstown on Lake Wakalipu to Martin's Bay on the West Coast with a man who was paid by Government £60 a year to carry the mails between Martin's Bay and Queenstown once a month. We carried our tent, blankets, and provisions on our backs, and the trip occupied five days. At that time there were only two families living at the bay—the mailman's and another man's—of course, not on speaking terms. Going to the bay the last fourteen miles was done by boat down Lake McKerrow and the river which runs out of it into the sea at Martin's Bay. On this occasion we were sailing down the lake in beautiful weather, close to the shore, and were about three miles from the settlement at Martin's Bay, where the mailman lived, when the other man, who was working in the bush near where we were, came down to the water's edge, leaving his work, and asked if there was anything in the mail for him? As it happened, the whole mail consisted of one newspaper addressed to the questioner. However, his neighbour, the mailman, stood up in the boat and shouted out, " If you come down to the post-office you can ascertain." And we went on without another word. The post-office, I may mention, was at his own house at Martin's Bay. I happened to be in the post-office that afternoon when the other man called, and I would rather not describe what was said and done. It took the man a good two hours to walk from where he hailed us to the post-office, and he did not know if he would get anything or not at the end of his journey. I can tell this much, at all events, he was not exactly pleased.

A Captain who has to go round New Zealand every three months, taking stores to the lighthouses and calling on the hermits and at the out-of-the-way settlements, has told me many a tale about this tendency to quarrel which exists among isolated settlers. Once when I was with him at a lighthouse where there were three men, the Captain was informed if he did not take one of the men away there would be murder before he came back. He left them to do as they pleased in the matter, and reported the happy family to the authorities. The Captain said, " I go to one of these settlements and meet, say, Jones. ' Good morning, Mr. Jones ; how's Mr. Brown ?' ' Don't ask me. If the Government knew the truth, they would take him away.' Next I meet Brown and say, ' Good morning, Mr. Brown, how's Mr. Smith ?' ' I don't know, and don't want to know anything about him.' Then, I say, ' Do you think Government knows what sort of man Jones is ?' and the answers comes, ' I am sure if they knew what a scoundrel.

he is, they would take him away.' Where there are women it is worse! I next meet Mrs. Smith, and say, 'Good morning, Mrs. Smith, how's your neighbour, Mrs. Brown?' 'Oh, please don't ask me; you don't suppose I have anything to do with those people. I hope I have not come down to that yet,' and Mrs. Brown, if I meet her, will say as much for Mrs. Smith." So said my friend the Captain, and he has had many years' experience now.

I once saw a pair of boots landed at one of these settlements. There were only two men at the settlement; one was away when we called, and the other came down to meet the boat. The mate, who took the boots ashore, asked where the other man was, as he had some boots for him. "Don't know," came the gruff answer. "Well, I'll leave the boots with you, and you can give them to him when he comes," joins in the mate. "No you won't, I won't take them," surlily persists the neighbour. "Well, I will put them down here, and you can tell him I left them" pleads the other. "You can put them where you like, but they will stop there for ever before I tell him anything about them," and thus the interesting dialogue closed.

CHAPTER XIV.

SUTHERLAND'S HOME.—A VISIT TO BOWEN FALLS.—STUPENDOUS SCENE.
— ANOTHER SUNSET IN MILFORD SOUND.—THE SOUND BY MOON-
LIGHT. — HARRISON COVE. — A NEAR GLIMPSE OF THE GLACIER
WORLD.—OUR BAKERS STILL A FAILURE.—THE DEPARTURE FROM
HARRISON COVE.—GOOD-BYE TO MILFORD SOUND.—M'KINNON'S
NEW TRACK TO LAKE TE ANAU.—A PARTING TRIBUTE TO MILFORD
SOUND SCENERY.

BUT to return to the " Rosa." After making the ship snug,
we landed and went up to Sutherland's house. The
house stands about 100 yards from and 50 feet above the
water, is of wood, well and strongly built, and contains three
rooms. The outer door was open and we went in, and found
everything very clean and neat, wood laid in the fireplace, and
many objects of interest tastefully arranged about the room.
On a table were several letters waiting for the Government
steamer, and a letter for her Captain, spread out for all to
read, stating that Sutherland and party were working on the
beach about two miles from Gate's Point, and asking the
Captain to leave them some provisions. It further requested
him to signal them as he passed the beach, so that they would
know when to come for them, as they were getting short.
This letter was dated October 19th, and as the Government
steamer had been round a week after that date she had
apparently not called.

Behind the dwelling-house were some outhouses, one of
which was fitted up with a forge, and contained a large and
good collection of tools, well kept. On a carpenter's bench
was an open diary, evidently meant to be seen, and it was
perused by some of the men. It was an account of Sutherland

and party's doings at Kaipo Beach, about six miles south of
Martin's Bay, and gave the dates of the washings up.   On
several occasions over 20 ozs., and on one over 40 ozs. were said
to have been obtained.   If gold was referred to I must say I
did not and do not believe anything of the sort.   If the state
ments in the diary were true, Sutherland would not be likely
to tell everybody by leaving his book in such a conspicuous
place, for he must have known that people would call there
during his absence.

There was a small garden at the back of the house, and in
it struggled for existence—with a mass of weeds and young
native undergrowth—roses, rhubarb, peas, and strawberry
plants.   The latter made a good show of fruit not yet ripe.

I went for a ramble through the bush, and climbed a good
way up the bed of a creek which comes down behind the
house, till I was stopped by a cascade with a fall of some 2,000
feet.   The bush was chiefly birch, with a good many rata or
ironwood trees, but there was not much large timber.   I had
a good look at a saddle-bird, a beautiful reddish-brown bird
with a dark bar across its back, and with red wattles.   It was
about the size of a thrush.   During my wanderings I obtained
magnificent views of wild mountain scenery, endless forest, and
still blue water, and I finally returned to the cutter at 6 p.m.

I then took the dingy and rowed to a convenient landing
place near Bowen Falls, about three-quarters of a mile pull
from the cutter.   After landing on a stony beach and hauling
up the dingy, I proceeded to inspect the falls.   I was unaccom-
panied by anyone.   I had to walk about half-a-mile to get at
them, my path being over rock-strewn and level rush-covered
ground.

Everything around was on a vast scale, but so clear is the
atmosphere in these regions that the visitor is constantly
taking mountains for hills and large waterfalls for small cascades.

Looking at the Bowen Falls from a distance of half-a-mile,
they do not seem to be much more than 100 feet in height;
but when you get close under them you realise that they are
as high as stated—viz., 540 feet unbroken fall.

All the way from the cutter I had been in more or less of a
drizzle, which ever thickened as I advanced.   As soon as I
had landed and long before I got to the fall itself, I was in
the midst of a thick cold rain, blown into me by a piercing

gale which seemed to emanate from the fall itself. I was speedily soaked to the skin. At length I stopped, for the simple reason that I could not well get any further.

I had traversed a rush-covered flat formed of *débris* brought down from the fall, and extending about 400 yards behind me. I now stood on a cliff at the edge of this formation about 20 yards from the fall itself, the river which flows from it washing the foot of the cliff about 30 feet below me. Around me danced a thick sheet of spray, hurried along by an icy cold wind, and filling my eyes and making vision extremely difficult. Every now and again this spray was so thick that I could see nothing. Vast as was the volume of falling water it was evidently sometimes much greater, for the ground I was standing on had recently been covered with running water. That this had been the case was clearly shewn by the fact that the tough rushes and reeds, which grew thickly on it and the flat I had traversed, were all crushed closed to the ground in one direction as if a heavy roller had passed over them.

Speech, even if I had had a companion with me, would have been impossible ; thought itself was almost so. Above, around, and under me rolled a never-ending peal of thunder, which shook the ground I stood upon. In front of me I beheld a vibrating, foaming, vapouring pillar of water over 500 feet high and 50 across, whose top I could see, but whose base was hidden by the hissing clouds of spray rising from the deep basin at its foot. Its roar deafened me, and I am sure that had a heavy piece of ordnance been discharged close to my ear I should not have heard the report. I was both delighted and awed with the majesty of the Bowen Falls. They far exceeded any description I had ever heard given of them.

As I returned to the dingy I noticed several boards nailed to trees containing names and dates. They were those of different ships which had visited the Sound, and were as follows :—

H.M.S. BLANCHE	...	...	...	1/10/74.
S.S. HINEMOA, Hooking	...	..	5/5/77.
,, HAWEA ...	...	...	...	30/12/77.
,, ROTORUA, Carey ...	...	...	6/1/79.
,, PENGUIN, Malcolm	...	...	1881.
,, WAIHORA ...	...	...	...	30/12/83.
NAPIER, 48 tons, Fisk ...	...	...	21/7/85.

I pulled back to the cutter, with a contented mind in a moist unpleasant body.

It was now sunset, and as evening came on the scene we gazed on was grandly serene, yet beautifully wild. It was perfectly calm, the silent waters reflecting and increasing the sunset glory of the mountains. The sunlight gilded the snow-capped peaks long after the shades of night had fallen on us. While the bushy mountain sides, valleys and lower peaks—notably one immediately under Mitre Peak—assumed a cobalt black tint, the outlines of the higher rocky masses stood out clear and distinct against the evening sky.

I have seen nothing to approach the scene we beheld since I gazed out of the darkness of the night at the 29,000 feet high peaks of Chan-Chin Jungla in the Himalayas, with their eternal snows still ruddy in the sunlight. The panorama spread before us reminded me irresistibly of the time when I had viewed mightier masses than those now looking us in the face—though not their equal in abrupt outline, and lacking the presence of water to reflect and magnify their terrible beauty. Gradually the last pink flush faded away from the highest snow, and the outlines only of the mountains could be distinguished against the sky in which the stars were now glimmering. We seemed to be floating at the bottom of a deep pit, for the countless bright stars overhead played with a dim light on the water around us. Presently a nearly full moon came climbing over the sharp black edge of a huge wall to the east, and as she rose threw over the scene a veil of silvery mist.

Early next morning there were no mountains to be seen. Masses of white mist obscured both mountain peak and wooded valley, but these dispersed as the sun mounted up in the heavens, though they still lingered about the snow-clad crests and dark-timbered slopes like beautiful, broken, pink and white fleeces.

We weighed anchor at half-past eight and stood down the sound, but it was rather curious progress that we made. We had a fresh, favourable breeze, and yet in spite of that the cutter constantly refused to answer her helm. Sometimes we went along sideways, and once or twice stern first. It was enough to make even a sailor swear, and at last our skipper lashed the helm, and told his vessel to "take her own road as she would not be guided." This extraordinary behaviour of the cutter was, I have no doubt, caused by strong under-currents, running contrary to the surface one, getting hold of the keel. In these sounds there is sometimes several feet deep of fresh water running out, and the heavier salt water from the sea running in under it. However, whether sideways or stern first, or as we ought to be, our progress was in the right direction down the sound. We had not gone very far though before the wind changed and commenced to blow a gale against us, so we shortened sail, and beating into Harrison Cove dropped anchor about ten o'clock.

Harrison Cove is a snug little harbour about a mile long and half-a-mile wide, three miles from Sutherland's on the right hand side going down, and from it are seen the very best views in Milford Sound, having snow and glaciers as prominent features. At no other point can a vessel anchor so close to the green ice and white snow.

From our anchorage, behind us, looking out of the cove, was a portion of Milford Sound, with the Mitre Peak heights as a background. To the right and left towered Sheerdown Cliffs, several thousand feet high, large portions of their rocky face devoid of bush but tinted green with fern and moss, and several cascades tumbling gracefully down them. In front of us was a small, narrow, timber-laden valley, the lower portion of it almost level, with a considerable sized glacier-fed stream meandering down its length.

This valley is enclosed by lofty snow-clad peaks, the hollows between them full of snow-covered ice and very close at hand. The highest points of Mount Pembroke, 6,800 feet, and Mount Tutoko, 9,042 feet, are respectively distant four and five miles. Anyone acquainted with mountain scenery can understand how mountains of such altitude, at such distances, will appear to tower above the observer.

There were several glaciers in view; one very fine one could be seen for several miles curling round and under a lofty, crescent-shaped peak, and its lower portions going well into the dark bush. I have no doubt but that an easy track could be cut to this glacier, and a visit to it would become a most enjoyable excursion for visitors coming to Milford. We landed as soon as we got to anchor, and the men started baking and washing.

I am sorry to have to record that the bakers do not improve, for they still turn out a compound which might serve as shot should our supply of that article run out. Yet it is not difficult to make eatable bread. Some months afterwards my brother-in-law and myself were alone for a considerable time in the wilderness, and we soon succeeded in turning out very fair bread, though having no greater advantages than those possessed by our merry Danes.

The rest of us went prospecting. Some of us penetrated a good distance up the river, the water of which was green in colour but clear as crystal. It flows over a bed of granite, and we found no trace of any mineral or quartz. There were, however, some considerable masses of white marble and boulders of heavy, green serpentine rock. We returned to the cutter at about 5 p.m.

At seven o'clock the skipper asked me to go fishing with him in the dingy, and I went. It was a stormy evening. Every now and again gusts of wind would sweep across the cove, making the cutter swing at her anchor, and then dying away leave the harbour with scarce a ripple on its surface. Out in the sound it was blowing a gale, and overhead dark heavy clouds drifted rapidly from the south-west. We pulled out of the cove and turned towards the mouth of the sound, keeping close to the shore. Here we found a space of half-a-mile or so where, by almost touching the land, we were sheltered from the wind but not the waves, for the latter came tumbling round a point which sheltered us, and rolled by several feet high. This we made our fishing ground for about an hour, though we constantly shifted our position; we had to keep a few yards only from the shore or we got no bottom, and then no fish.

It was a wild scene, tossing on the big waves in our little boat at the foot of the mighty Sheerdown with its 5,000 feet of sheer rocky cliff. Its crest, when we looked up, actually seemed to overhang us. On the other side of the wind-driven sound, a mile-and-a-half across, rose a similar cliff with dark, angry-looking clouds resting on its brow. The black-browed skipper was quite in keeping with the surroundings, and seemed in his element, for he opened his broad shoulders and pulled his little craft into the crestless waves as if he loved them. He was in good humour, and consequently made good company. We caught a few blue cod and one trumpeter, and pulled back to the cutter in the dusk. It was extremly cold, and a piercing wind swept in gusts from the snow-crowned heights with which the sound is land-locked. As night came on snow began to fall on the mountains, and icy rain upon us.

Pat was anxious to spend some time in Harrison Cove and

explore the valley, glaciers, &c., and I regret we did not, but the majority were desirous to proceed to Big Bay without further loss of time, and the idea was not entertained.

Next morning was Sunday, the 12th December, fine, but very cold. The mountains looked superb in their coating of fresh snow which came down to within 2,000 feet of sea level—*i.e.*, considerably below the bush-line. We remained at anchor all day. It was a beautiful evening, and at sunset I took the dingy and pulled about the cove, silently admiring the golden glory of the scene.

At midnight we weighed anchor, it being a fine cloudless night with the moon nearly full, and her silvery rays lighting up the mountain peaks with talismanic effect. We glided out of Harrison Cove, helped by a light night wind which blew with an icy touch down the valley from the glaciers. As we got into the sound the wind died away, and the weather soon changed, for rain commenced to fall. It took four hours to cover two miles, and it was eight o'clock in the morning before we dropped anchor once more in Anita Bay.

We had not been anchored long before Jack the dog, who had been left behind when we were last here, was swimming round the cutter, yelping to attract attention. Tom, the sailor, gave a howl of delight when he saw him, and yelled out, " Our Jack's come home to day," a refrain from a song he was very fond of singing, and which, as far as I am aware, exhausted his vocal *réportoire*. He soon had Jack safe on board.

All that day and the next it blew a gale, with intermittent showers. The weather cleared up on the evening of the second day, and at six in the morning of the 15th December we weighed anchor and sailed out of Milford Sound. This time we did not have to put back, and so we had finished with Milford Sound at last.

Had we foreseen how long the weather would have detained us there we should have landed tents and stores, and explored some of the valleys about the district; but expecting the weather would permit us to sail next day always kept us more or less confined to the cutter.

The chief sights of Milford to one visiting it in a steamer are, first—Mount Pembroke to the left; then the narrows, with their 4,000 feet cliffs on either side; Sterling Falls, as you emerge from them, to the left; next, on the same side comes Harrison Cove, encircled with its sky-piercing peaks and

dazzling glaciers; to the right will now be seen the remarkable outline of Mitre Peak, and as the vessel proceeds Hawrenny Peaks will also come in view in the same direction.
Bowen Falls will be observed for some miles ahead before the
anchorage off Sutherland's house is reached; and the traveller,
in fact, is encircled by views any one of which would suffice,
either in Europe or America, annually to attract crowds of
tourists to the spot.

I have several times visited Milford Sound since, and on one
occasion had a trip to Lake Ada. This lake is about four
miles from Sutherland's, and we went partly by boat, and then
some three miles along a good track cut through the bush. The
lake is four miles long and half-a-mile wide, and is shut
in on both sides by mountains rising as much as 6,000 feet.
The walk to the lake through the bush is very pleasant, and
the ferns which cover the ground like a carpet are, many of
them, rare. Splendid glimpses are from time to time obtained
through openings in the forest of mountain peaks many thousand feet above the traveller.

The track recently discovered by Mr. M'Kinnon from Milford to Lake Te Anau is tolerably easy, and when finished it
is said that ladies will be able to traverse it with comfort. It
passes Lake Ada and the Sutherland Falls about eight miles
from the head of the lake. These falls have been measured
and photographed. They descend 1,900 feet in three leaps.
From the falls the track rises over a saddle, and drops into
the Clinton River valley; then follows down the Clinton River
till Lake Te Anau is reached. Te Anau is a beautiful body of
water, the largest in the South Island, for it covers an area of
132 square miles, and is about 36 miles long. Its scenery on
the western side, where several arms penetrate far into the
mountains, very much resembles that of the sounds. It is
accessible from Dunedin or Invercargill by coach and rail.

A good traveller will, when McKinnon's track is finished,
be able to go from Te Anau to Sutherland's Falls in one day,
and there is no doubt but that this track, which connects the
finest lake scenery in New Zealand with the unique scenery
of the West Coast Sounds, will before long be much frequented
by tourists. I think, however, that the saddle between Milford and Te Anau could be more easily reached from the head
of George Sound than from Milford.

Milford and several of the sounds are a favourite resort of

large porpoises—called sea cows. They can be seen almost any day rolling about by the hundred.

Every time I go into Milford its marvellous scenery impresses me more and more. One of the most wonderful effects of light and shadow I ever saw was when coming down Milford at night in a steamer. It was full moon, and we left the head of the sound at midnight and steamed out to sea. The base of the mountains was steeped in darkness, but a flood of silver light rested on the ridges and peaks, and the sheen of the water could be seen glistening like a radiant thread between two black-bottomed, silver-topped walls. The glowing mountain peaks seemed indeed to be floating on a dark mist.

I take the following from my diary, and thus conclude my description of the West Coast Sounds of New Zealand, an account of the wild country to the north, where I have spent some years in the work of exploration, must be left to another time :—

" A scene of stupendous beauty : I saw, as it were, silvered dome and mitred peak resting on darkness ; through this darkness trailed a streak of silver, and down this silver trail we passed, on and on, under black cliffs that hung over us, like portals of eternal darkness, like the mouths of huge, endless, hellish caverns, breathing eternal gloom !—home of the spirit of night. And above this stupendous mass of obscurity float palaces of light, veils of luminous mist, pinnacles of topaz, lakes of pure white marble, and domes of fairy silver. It falls behind us, and we are out on the moon-silvered sea. The huge mountains sink and sink till they look like cloud-banks on the horizon. The southern swell moves silently past, making us stagger as we pace the deck. The land-wind strikes cold, and as the sounds are left behind, we turn in."

THE END.

LONDON : PRINTED BY THOBURN AND CO., 136, SALISBURY SQUARE, FLEET SQUARE, E.C.

CPSIA information can be obtained at www.ICGtesting.com
Printed in the USA
LVOW08*1522140813

347902LV00005B/118/P